D1256879

Chelewa, Chelewa
The Dilemma of Teenage Girls

Edited by
Zubeida Tumbo-Masabo
and Rita Liljeström

Nordiska Afrikainstitutet , 1994

(The Scandinavian Institute of African Studies)

LIBRARY, ST. LAWRENCE UNIVERSITY
CANTON, NEW YORK 13617

HQ
799
.T35
C54
1994

This book is published with support from The Swedish Agency for
Research Cooperation with Developing Countries (SAREC).

Note: The photographs in this book do **not** depict any of the persons
described in the text.

Indexing terms
Sociology
Demography
Girls
Family
Education
Marriage
Sexuality
Pregnancy
Abortion
Tanzania

Cover: Adriaan Honcoop
Cover photo: *Two smiling adolescent girls*, David Dahmén,
Bazaar Bildbyrå, Stockholm
Copyediting: Peter Colenbrander
Layout: Anders Suneson and Per-Anders Agdler
Printed in Sweden by Tryckeribolaget, Östersund 1994
© The authors and Nordiska Afrikainstitutet, 1994
ISBN 91-7106-354-4

SEP 26 1997

Contents

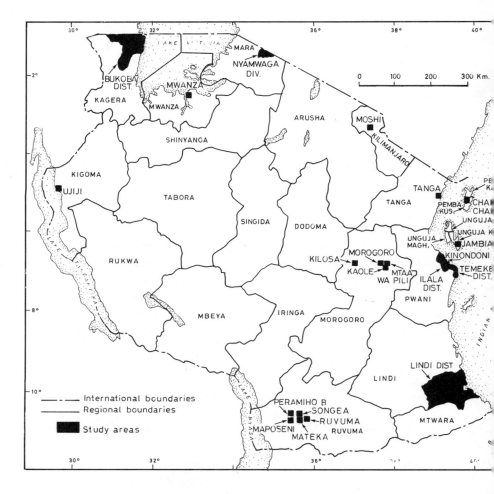

MAP OF TANZANIA SHOWING STUDY AREAS

Chapter 2
Kilimanjaro (Moshi)
Tanga (town)
Mwanza (town)
Pemba (Chake Chake)

Chapter 3
Zanzibar (Jambiani)
Mara (Tarime district – Nyamwaga division)

Chapter 4
Morogoro (Morogoro district – Mtaa wa Pili and
Kaole villages)
Ruvuma (Songea district – Ruvuma, Mateka,
Peramiho B and Maposeni villages, Songea town)

Chapter 5
Lindi (Lindi rural district)

Chapter 6
Kigoma (Ujiji)
Dar es Salaam (all three districts)

Chapter 7
Dar es Salaam (all three districts)
Morogoro (Morogoro town and Kilosa)

Chapter 8
Kagera (district)
Dar es Salaam (all three districts)

Preface

Zubeida Tumbo-Masabo

This book is the result of studies conducted by the Teenage Girls and Reproductive Health Study Group. We are ten researchers drawn from two women's groups at the University of Dar es Salaam: the Women's Research and Documentation Project (WRDP), and the Institute of Development Studies Women's Study Group (IDSWSG), and have been joined by our mentor, Rita Liljeström, professor at the Swedish Council for Research in the Humanities and Social Sciences; she works at the University of Gothenburg.

The Teenage Girls and Reproductive Health Study Group was formed in 1989–90 and was awarded funding by the Swedish Agency for Research Cooperation with Developing Countries (SAREC), which has supported all our activities to date. Our principal goal is to conduct studies that emphasize the socio-cultural and economic aspects of reproductive health. We are now in the middle of the second phase of our work which includes some studies on teenage boys.

This book is based on the research conducted during 1990–91 and 1991–92. Our aim has been to reflect on the work that we have done and present research reports that can reach a larger readership.

The first part of the title, *Chelewa, Chelewa,* is drawn from a Kiswahili proverb, *Chelewa chelewa utamkuta mtoto si wako,* which means that if you do not take proper and timely action, you will end up a loser. Many things will thus be spoiled because of such delay. The proverb is very appropriate to the situation of teenage girls in Tanzania.

Although our team has worked very hard to produce this book, we have not done it alone. In order to sharpen our understanding of the issues involved, we selected a group of resource people from different fields related to our study and asked for their help. They participated in the workshops that we organized at different stages of our research and writing. At our first workshop, held at Bahari Beach Hotel from 30 July to 3 August 1990, we examined research methodologies. In addition to our mentor, the following resource people took part: Dr. Comoro, Department of Sociology, Dr. Samuel Chambua, Institute of Development Studies, and Dr. Ernest Urassa, Department of Gynaecology and Obstetrics – all at the University of Dar es Salaam; Priscilla Ole-Kambainei, Ministry of National Education; and Mr. Cletus Mkai, Bureau of Statistics. Also in attendance were two members from WRDP and IDSWSG respectively: Anna Nkebukwa and Rose Shayo.

The second workshop, during which the draft reports were reviewed, was held at Mommela Lodge, Arusha, from 22–27 June 1992. With the exception of Dr. Comoro, who was replaced by Dr. Masanja of the same department, Ms. Ole-Kambainei, who could not attend, and Ms. Kassimoto, Ministry of Community Development, Women's Affairs and Children, who joined the resource team, the rest of the resource persons have been permanently involved.

The third workshop reviewed the draft chapters for this book. It was held at Mikumi Wildlife Lodge, Morogoro, from 4–9 January 1993. The group benefited from the comments made by the core group of resource persons: Drs. Urassa, Chambua and Masanja, Mr. Mkai and Ms. Kassimoto who were at this stage joined by Mr. Moses Tuguta, Ministry of Education, and Hanna Olsson from Sweden.

The drafts were then reviewed by the authors and edited by Rita Liljeström, Grace Puja and Zubeida Tumbo-Masabo, with the assistance of Ebenezar Osei-Kofi, University of Kumasi, Ghana, and Birgit Jörn, University of Gothenburg, who did the final typing and corrections. The initial drafts were diligently typed by some of the authors themselves and by Mr. Marombwa, Department of Statistics, Ms. Judith Stephen and Ms. Rukia Mwabba, Institute of Kiswahili Research, all at the University of Dar es Salaam.

We would like to thank all of those who contributed to making the research and writing a success. These include the research authorities at the universities of Dar es Salaam and Gothenburg, respondents, friends and colleagues, and the two women's groups who showed great interest in the work we were doing; WRDP organized a seminar which members of both WRDP and IDSWSG attended to comment on our research. However, our highest gratitude goes to our families who have had to tolerate our extremely busy schedules during this whole undertaking. We are also highly indebted to SAREC for supporting our efforts to highlight the sociological issues of teenage reproductive health by funding us and by organizing regional conferences for all sectors dealing with similar programmes in Southern Africa.

Zubeida Tumbo-Masabo
Coordinator

1. Facts about and images of teenage girls in Tanzania

Samuel E.Chambua, Magdalena Kamugisha Rwebangira, Rita Liljeström, and Ernest J. N. Urassa

How come there is such great international interest in teenage girls in the Third World? One explanation could lie in demographic factors. Teenage girls are the mothers of tomorrow and they should reproduce less than their mothers and grandmothers did. This implies a break with the past, when women were respected for being fertile and giving birth to many children.

Consequently, the National Population Policy in Tanzania, intends, among other things, "to reduce the incidence of pregnancies among women below the age of eighteen years" by means of the integrated maternal and child health and family planning program-mes. Another measure to be adopted is "to raise the minimum age at marriage for girls to eighteen years" (para. 61, section iii).

Demographic characteristics

Girls in the age group ten to nineteen years old have increased from about 10 per cent of all women in 1967 to about 24 per cent in 1988. Projections based on the 1988 census figures indicate that this figure will apparently decline to a level of about 22 per cent after the year 2000 (Census publications 1967, 1968 and 1988).

Several population censuses have been conducted at intervals of about ten years. Additionally, a number of surveys as well as case studies have been carried out in Tanzania at household level. Invariably, demographic and socio-economic data have been solicited. However, analysis has often been disaggregated by sex using broad age-groups. Furthermore, teenage girls have hardly been considered as a specific group for the purpose of analysis. Only when age-classifications, such as ten to fourteen and fifteen to nineteen years, have been adopted, may the analysis be properly focused.

Age-specific mortality rates

Age-specific mortality rates have been computed by sex. The rates are higher for boys than for girls but both declined between 1978 and 1988. Furthermore, the figures show that those between fifteen and nineteen are at greater risk of dying than the ten to fourteen year olds.

Table 1. *Age-specific mortality rates, 1978–88*

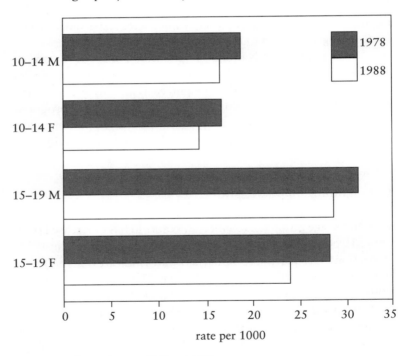

rate per 1000

Source: Population Census, 1978 and 1988

For females, this could be due to reproductive complications. Moreover, risks from accidents increase with age for both sexes.

Evolution of population policy

Up to about the mid-1970s, many African governments held that their national populations were rather small and they consequently expressed a desire for a larger population (Ekanem, 1988:4). During the 1980s, however, there occurred a change of attitude among African governments in favour of lowering the rates of population growth. Whereas in 1979 eight African countries had policies to raise their annual population growth rates, by 1987 only three countries had such policies; the number of countries with policies to lower their population growth increased from fifteen to twenty-seven between 1979 and 1987; and the number of countries which formulated policies aimed at stabilizing their estimated population growth rates increased from zero to twenty during the same period, i.e., 1979–87 (Ekanem, 1988). This change in attitude took place at a time when many sub-Saharan African countries were facing severe socio-economic crises which had begun in the mid-1970s. These crises have, *inter alia*, made governments increasingly aware of their nations' inability to provide basic needs, such as food and social amenities, to rapidly growing populations.

Tanzania is similar to many sub-Saharan African countries in the revolution that its population policy has undergone. There has been a change from hypersensitivity and virtual hostility up to the end of the 1970s to attempting to formulate an explicit population policy after the mid-1980s (Kamuzora, 1989; Chambua; 1991). The thrust of the National Population Policy (NPP) of the Tanzania – which was adopted in early 1992 – is to reduce the population growth rate through fertility reduction. According to the 1988 census, the annual population growth rate from 1978 to 1988 was 2.8 per cent while the total fertility rate (TFR) was 6.4 in 1988.

Thus, the evolution of population policy in Tanzania went through two distinct phases: firstly, an implicit policy characterized by resistance to family planning, family-life education and/or opposition to the whole idea of population policy; secondly, an explicit policy characterized by the encouragement of family planning, family-life education and the integration of population concerns into development planning.

Phase 1: Implicit policy hostile to explicit policy

The government of Tanzania has always recognized the role that demographic factors play in the achievement of the country's goals of socio-economic development. However, up to the mid-1980s, Tanzania's development plans treated demographic factors and trends as more or less given (i.e., independent variables) and sought to assimilate them into other development activities.

During this period of implicit population policy, however, the government had to deal with various issues pertaining to population-cum-development, especially in the areas of settlement, rural-urban migration, education and health. These included census-taking every ten years, the settlement schemes of the early 1960s, the Ujamaa Villages and Villagization programmes of the late 1960s to mid-1970s; the expansion of primary education and the subsequent adoption of the Universal Primary Education (UPE) policy in 1976; provision of adult education and expansion of health facilities to reduce mortality; the launching of the integrated Maternal and Child Health (MCH) programme in 1974 in which family planning/child spacing (FP/CS) services were and are incorporated; and the various measures taken during the past three decades to reduce rural-urban migration. These measures notwithstanding,

...nowhere in development plans or in other government pronouncements is population treated as a separated coherent entity...this was at least deliberate...To a large extent this reluctance seems to be concerned with fertility reduction. (UNFPA, 1979:21)

Phase II: Evolution of an explicit population policy

The evolution of an explicit population policy can be traced back to 1969 when President Nyerere urged Tanzanians to match child-bearing with their ability to take good care of their children.

It is very good to increase our population, because our country is large and there is plenty of unused land. But...these...extra people every year will be babies in arms, not workers. They will have to be fed...for very many years. It is for this reason that it is important for

human beings to put emphasis on caring for children and the ability to look after them properly, rather than thinking only about the numbers of children and the ability to give birth. (Nyerere, 1969:xii)

The significance of this statement is that though it did not immediately lead to an explicit population policy, it, nonetheless, gave legitimacy to UMATI–the Family Planning Association of Tanzania (Chambua, 1991).

Another harbinger of an explicit policy came in 1978–79 when the government made the provision that "for a person with children there will...be a refund of tax calculated at the rate of Tshs. 10 per child per month, up to a maximum of four children" (Minister of Finance, 1978). Other employment-related benefits have also been limited to four children to date.

From 9–13 January 1984 the Second African Population Conference was held in Arusha, Tanzania. The conference adopted a ninety-three-point document called the Kilimanjaro Programme of Action on Population which urged governments to integrate population variables in development plans and

...ensure the availability and accessibility of family planning services to all couples or individuals seeking such services freely or at subsidized prices.

This conference was held at a time when Tanzania was in a deep socio-economic crisis which had begun in 1978–79. The growth rate of the GDP was 0.5 per cent, 0.6 per cent and 2.4 per cent per annum in 1980–81, 1981–82 and 1982–83 respectively. Shortages of virtually everything were the order of the day and many of the country's achievements during the 1960s and 1970s were seriously eroded. This was followed by a number of population projects in the fields of family-life education, MCH, information, and population awareness seminars for the public, party and government officials and leaders. These seminars and projects were externally funded. The culmination of all this was a directive in 1986 from the ruling party, Chama Cha Mapinduzi (CCM), to the government to formulate an explicit population policy. By 1988, a draft policy document was ready for dissemination and public discussion. This occurred and, after taking into consideration the views of the public and after subsequent revision, the NPP was finally adopted by the government in February 1992.

The National Population Policy (NPP)

The principal objective of the explicit NPP is "to reinforce national development through developing available resources, in order to improve the quality of life of the people" (URT, 1992:para. 20). Other policy goals to be emphasized, are, *inter alia*:

To strengthen family planning services in order to promote the health and welfare of the family, the community and the nation and...reduce the rate of population growth. (para. 22, section iii)

To promote and strengthen proper youth upbringing and growth including the creation of an environment that will allow optimal development of their various talents. (section vii)

In order to achieve the aims of the NPP, the goals of various population programmes are to include the following:

To make family planning means and services easily accessible so as to reduce maternal and child mortality. (para. 55, section iv)

To prepare young people, before marriage, through proper upbringing and the provision of family life education... (section v)

To educate the public on the benefits of women marrying and bearing children after the age of eighteen years. (section vi)

and,

To improve women's status in society by reviewing existing laws in areas where their rights and those of children are undermined within the family, community and places of work... (section vii)

Will she be better prepared, have fewer children and know her rights?
Daily News, Dar es Salaam

It should be noted from our discussion that the key word for the NPP is "integration" of population into development plans and programmes. That is, population variables and goals should be made endogenous and not exogenous to development planning. Furthermore, the hostility, hypersensitivity, and reluctance regarding family planning, family-life education, and fertility limitation seem to have faded, at least officially. Finally, the formulation and review, coordination, planning, monitoring and evaluation of population policy and activities in the country will be done by the President's Office–the Planning Commission.

Reproductive health policies

A second explanation for the interest in teenage girls comes from the international health community

which has focused attention on maternal and child health problems, and has viewed women's health problems primarily as these relate to their reproductive roles. This constituency has tended to view the woman only as a mother. And since poor maternal outcome and child health is directly linked to pregnancy outcome, the woman has been used as a vehicle for improving child survival. (Pauchauri, 1993)

However, women's reproductive health is not only a medical concern, but has, for instance, to do with the reproductive roles of women and men (Kabeer, 1992), the social regulation of the affiliation of children and child maintenance (Bruce, 1992), and with informing teenagers how to prevent unwanted pregnancies.

Soon social scientists took part in research on reproductive health, including the team working on the present book. However, the position of teenage girls still remains unclear, because their marital status evokes controversy. Today, a growing community of women activists draws attention to the importance of women's empowerment and reproductive rights. In the local context, where we have studied teenage girls from a reproductive health perspective, the message of empowerment looks like a remote dream, but is nonetheless urgent.

The age of marriage

In some parts of Tanzanian society, teenagers are given away to men for marriage at menarche, which may occur as early as the age of twelve years. Sometimes the man is old enough to be the girl's grandfather and usually the teenager has no say in the choice of husband. These traditions basically assume that a woman is mature when she has had menarche.

The singulate mean age at marriage has been steadily increasing since 1967. However, while on average more men marry above the age of nineteen years, more women marry within the teenage group. More than half the women who have ever married have done so by the age of seventeen (59.29 per cent).

Table 2. *Percentage distribution of ever-married women by age at first marriage*

Age at 1st marriage	Per cent	Cumulative per cent
less than 12 years	2.68	2.68
12 "	3.34	6.02
13 "	5.92	11.94
14 "	10.21	22.15
15 "	13.14	35.29
16 "	12.23	47.52
17 "	11.77	59.29
18 "	9.96	69.25
19 "	7.64	76.89
20 and above	23.11	100.00

Source: Bureau of Statistics, Ministry of Finance and Economic Planning, National Demographic Sample Survey of Tanzania (1973), Vol. I, table 2090.

At the age of nineteen years, more than three-quarters of the ever-married women in this country were married at least once. Besides, marriage first occurs very early. Six per cent of the ever-married women are married by the age of twelve years.

The age at first marriage increases as the number of years of education increase. However, there has been a tendency to delay the first marriage even for those with no or very little education. Economic hardships may be assumed to contribute towards an increase in age at first marriage, irrespective of social status.

Table 3. *Median age at first marriage by number of years of education for women aged 20–24 and 25–29*

| Years of Education | Age-group | |
	20–24	25–29
-	17.06	16.90
1–4	17.28	17.20
5–8	17.94	18.00
9–13	19.39	20.90

Source: Bureau of Statistics, Ministry of Finance and Economic Planning, National Demographic Sample Survey of Tanzania (1973), Vol. II, table 2093.

Differences in culture, religion, etc., have been shown to affect age at first marriage. The figure below shows analyses from six different parts of Tanzania: Chaga (north eastern), Haya (north western), Nyakusa (south western), Makonde (southern), Zaramo (eastern, coastal) and Gogo (central).

Table 4. *Median age at first marriage by ethnic group*

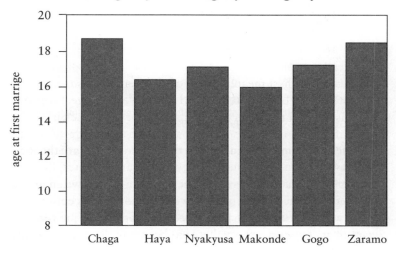

The chapters below on schoolgirl pregnancies and arranged marriages as well as the study of the Mwera of Lindi, all illustrate the risks related to early marriages on the one hand, and to the widening gap between puberty and marriage on the other.

Some of the repercussions of early marriage can be quite traumatic. For example, more than 2.5 per cent of the evermarried women of fifteen to nineteen years have experienced divorce, separation or death of a spouse. And 5 per cent have remarried at least once.

Table 5. *Ever-married women by age-group and number of marriages (per cent)*

Age–group	Number of times married				
	1	2	3	4–8	Total
15-19	94.8	4.3	0.5	0.4	100
20–24	88.5	10.0	1.0	0.5	100
25–29	81.9	15.2	2.0	0.9	100
30–34	75.8	18.8	3.9	1.5	100
35–39	72.3	20.0	5.3	2.4	100
40–44	70.2	21.6	5.5	2.7	100
45–49	71.2	20.4	5.9	2.5	100

Source: Bureau of Statistics, Ministry of Economic Planning, National Demographic Sample Survey of Tanzania (1973) vol. II, table 2100

Women who were below the age of twelve when their first marriages took place had the lowest mean number of children. However, the highest mean number of children born is for women who first married between twelve and sixteen years of age. From this data, it is apparent that very early marriages expose the girl to the risk of infertility. At the same time, marriage in the mid-teens results in high fertility compared to other age groups (Bureau of Statistics, 1973).

About 95 per cent of currently married women of between fifteen and nineteen years are not using any method of contraception. For the few women using some form of contraception, 1.4 per cent are reported to be using the pill. Traditional methods, especially abstinence, were practised by 1.7 per cent and withdrawal by 1.4 per cent (Tanzania Demographic and Health Survey, 1991–92).

Furthermore, data on the singulate mean at first birth indicate that women in rural areas give birth at an earlier age than their counterparts in urban areas. Also, the data indicate that more women are now postponing their first births compared to the 1970s.

Pregnancy complications

For most of these young girls, pubertal growth is still progressing. They have neither reached mental nor full physical maturity. These girls have not had the opportunity to attend school and are, therefore, subject to only traditional rules and practices of childbirth. The societies where teenage marriages and pregnancies are common are usually poor and have limited access to medical facilities.

Teenage pregnancies mean competition between the young growing mothers and the foetus in her womb for scarce food and other nutrients. This often leads to stunted growth of the woman and general malnutrition. Both maternal and infant mortality rates are high in teenage pregnancies. Teenagers constitute 22 per cent of women who deliver at Muhimbili Medical Centre and account for 17 per cent of maternal mortality in Dar es Salaam (Urassa, 1994).

As has already been noted, teenagers account for 22 per cent of the total deliveries at Muhimbili Medical Centre.

Table 6. *Age distributions of deliveries at Muhimbili Medical Centre 1990–91*

Age	Number	Per cent
10–19	1,913	21.6
20–29	4,249	48.1
30–39	2,173	24.6
40–49	505	5.7
Total	8,840	100

They, however, experience more than their share of morbidity. Tradition and custom do not favour them either. Teenagers are subject to special complications, some of which arise from their youthfulness. About 40 per cent of teenagers, as compared to 15 per cent of older women, were not married. This has special implications for pre-natal care, maternal nutrition and decision-making on various aspects of care. Teenagers usually attend ante-natal clinics late and anaemia is likely to remain undetected until the end of the course of pregnancy. In some cases, teenage pregnancies may not be revealed until the girls suffer from severe anaemia. Often the anaemia has been treated with local medicines without success and the hospital is the last resort. The competition between the growing mother and her developing foetus for iron and other food nutrients leaves the mother malnourished and anaemic. Severe anaemia is more prevalent among teenagers. A review of a thousand consecutive deliveries shows that teenagers account for one-third of all cases of severe anaemia (Hb less than 6.5).

Hypertensive diseases, particularly eclampsia, are known to be more common among young mothers. Ninety per cent of women suffering from eclampsia, but only 51 per cent of all women, are teenagers (see table below). They also report late for check-ups and hence the blood pressure problem is not detected early. In this review, the average stage at which teenagers reported for their first ante-natal visit was thirty weeks, compared to twenty-eight for older women. The prevalence of eclampsia among teenagers in Tanzania was reported to be 9.9 per 1,000 deliveries as compared to 6.5 per 1,000 in older women (Kapesa, 1985).

Teenage women tend to experience difficulty in labour and are more likely to have assisted deliveries. Five out of nine women with contracted pelvises are teenagers.

Table 7. *Distribution of the top four causes of morbidity in 1,000 consecutive births at Muhimbili Medical Centre 1990–91*

Type of morbidity	Age 10–19	Age 20–44	Total
Hypertension/ Eclampsia	19	18	37
Anaemia	4	8	12
Haemorrhage (APH&PPH)	2	11	13
Obstructed labour (& Caesarean section)	5	9	14
Total morbidity	30	46	76

Obstructed labour often leads to foetal death and damage to maternal soft tissues. Urinary and/or fecal incontinence is often a result of difficult labour. About 95 per cent of all women admitted at Muhimbili Medical Centre with vesical vaginal fistula or rectal vaginal fistula are teenagers who have had difficulty in labour. These women often lead very miserable lives. They become social outcasts because they smell of urine and/or faeces and are often divorced.

Unwanted pregnancies

In Tanzania, tradition and culture attach great weight to having a baby and there are no acceptable ways of dealing with an unwanted pregnancy. Consequently, the National Population Policy and the law do not regard abortion as one of the methods of achieving family planning; indeed, it remains a criminal offence. The psychological disturbance resulting from the conflict between a society that demands the preservation of pregnancy at any cost and the wishes of the younger teenager who is not ready to bear children is profound.

Of the women who had abortions at Muhimbili gynaecological wards, 54 per cent were teenagers and of those with septic induced abortions, 65 per cent were teenagers. Current studies indicate that abortion is a major cause of maternal death among teenagers. An ongoing study of Ilala district, Dar es Salaam, reveals that 15 per cent of maternal deaths are due to septic abortions and one-third of these occur among teenagers. The morbidity due to septic abortions among desperate teenagers who have unplanned pregnancies is reflected in the number of women who become infertile early in their marriages. Tubal block is a principal cause of failure to conceive and about 25 per cent of these women have a history of teenage septic abortion. Chronically painful menstruation and painful coitus following abortion often make the lives of these women very miserable.

Table 8. *Age distributions of abortion cases at Muhimbili gynaecological wards, January–June 1992*

Type of abortion	Age distributions		Total
	10–19	19–45	
Spontaneous (per cent)	34 (46.6)	39 (53.4)	73
Septic (per cent)	35 (64.8)	19 (35.2)	54
Total	69 (54)	58 (46)	127

Note: Teenage girls have significantly more septic abortions than other women X2=22.545, P less than 0.001

Lack of policy and facilities to deal with unwanted pregnancies leads to septic abortions. This is not only an important cause of death among teenagers, but it causes chronic morbidity and marital disharmony in survivors who may have become infertile.

Targeting teenage girls

Many young women grow up in a situation where they are dominated by much older men. They do not get opportunities for education and/or employment. Moreover, they are not given the chance to decide on what happens to and affects their lives. They, therefore, feel socially inferior. Much of the morbidity that occurs in the reproductive life of young women in Tanzania can be attributed to the low status accorded to women, especially when they have fallen pregnant so young and have no say about when to have the next baby, how many babies to have and even where to go for care during pregnancy.

In the ongoing social construction of "the teenage girl", the population issue and the medical risks associated with early pregnancies are the main elements that define her as a problem. Therefore, all pregnancies below the age of eighteen are not considered desirable. In societies where marriage at the outset of menarche has been practised for centuries, this must sound incongruous. Yet, emphasis on the role of malnutrition, utter poverty and poor medical facilities would shift attention from the upper teens to gender and economic policies. Besides, although aspirations to provide girls with education and jobs are good social reasons for delaying marriage and maternity, those opportunities are simply not available to most girls. The teenage girl becomes socially defined by all the movements and individuals who advocate her emancipation and her reproductive rights – her empowerment, as they say today. Their images necessarily allegorize her as a victim, undernourished, poor, neglected, oppressed, expelled, exploited, seduced and silenced.

The eagerness of international organizations to promote their case has resulted in a "pathologization of the teenage girl" (Phoenix, 1991) thus overlooking the existence of all the young mothers in their upper teens (16–19) who are healthy and able to take care of their newborn children. However, these tendencies are not limited to teenagers in the Third World. "The teenage girl problem" is partially imported from Western societies. In countries like Britain, not to mention the United States, teenage motherhood is a cause for concern. There are many components in this concern; one is "he

Ambiguity is in the eye of the beholder.
Daily News, Dar es Salaam

moral panic" aroused by youthful sexuality, and the ambiguity of adolescense as a status. Others are the concern about the consequences for mother and child and the awareness that early motherhood seems to be most common among the poor. Poverty easily gets mixed up with age, as Ann Phoenix notes:

Although early motherhood is associated with poverty there is no evidence that motherhood in the teenage years causes poverty. In most cases there is no reason to believe that their situation would improve as they got older. Although teenage women who become mothers are often believed to constitute a social problem, it may be more accurate to view them as a group of mothers with problems— often not of their own making—who are struggling against the odds. Most fare well under difficult circumstances. (Phoenix, 1991:253)

According to Phoenix, the negative social construction placed upon early motherhood provides the context within which teenage pregnancies are discussed. Therefore, researchers tend to start with the assumption that early motherhood is a social problem, and end in reinforcing popular beliefs instead of providing evidence of all those teenage mothers who succeed as well as women over twenty do.

We do not argue that there is no truth in all those images. Why would we otherwise write this book or involve ourselves in research on teenage girls and their reproductive health? Yet what worries us, besides the tendency to exaggerate her plight, is that we all seem to treat her as a target and not as an actor in her own right. We tend to speak on her behalf, not giving her a chance to raise her own voice. We locate her in our scenarios. They determine our interpretations. While working on the topic of the teenage girl, we have encountered a few of those well-known international problem-scenarios which "frame" the teenage girl. They become replicated in hundreds of studies. Is it possible to go beyond them?

What would happen if we instead constructed "the old men's problem" and brought it into the limelight? Maybe it would throw more light on the teenage girls' difficulties than further studies on them would do. What would be the outcome if we approached the population problem and the medical risks of reproduction by focusing similar long-term attention on "men's uncontrolled desire"?

In exploring various options, one becomes aware of how safe teenage girls are as targets, perfect for projecting other people's problems onto.

References

Bruce, Judith, 1992, *Reproductive Choice: the Responsibilities of Men and Women*, Day of Dialogue on Population and Feminist Perspectives. London: The Population Council.

Bureau of Statistics, 1973, Ministry of Finance and Economic Planning, National Demographic Sample Survey of Tanzania, Vol.I.

Bureau of Statistics, 1973, Ministry of Finance and Economic Planning, National Demographic Sample Survey of Tanzania, Vol.II.

Chambua, S.E., 1991, *In-depth Assessment of Population and Development Planning Activities in Selected African Countries: Tanzania case study*. Research Report, Nairobi: Prepared for ILO.

Ekanem, I.I., 1988, "African Population Policies: Formulation and Implementation in the 1970s and 1980s". Paper presented at the African Population Conference, Dakar, Senegal.

Kabeer, Naila, 1992, *Overview of the Population/Feminist Divide*, Day of Dialogue on Population and Feminist Perspectives. London: The Population Council.

Kamuzora, C.L., 1989, *The Evolution of Policy on Fertility in Tanzania: Drawing on, and Influence of International Experience*. Mimeo. Demographic Planning Unit, Dar es Salaam University.

Kapesa, A.T., 1985, "The Pattern of Eclampsia in Dar es Salaam", *Journal of Obstetrics and Gynaecology of Eastern and Central Africa*, 4, 77–9.

Nyerere, J.K., 1969, in *United Republic of Tanzania. Second Five Year Plan for Economic and Social Development*. Vol. 1, Dar es Salaam. Government Printer.

Pauchauri, Saroj, 1993, *The Problem*, Population Planning. Seminar 410, New Delhi.

Phoenix, Ann, 1991, *Young Mothers?* Cambridge: Polity Press.

Tanzania, 1991, *The Informal Sector Survey*.

United Nations Fund for Population Activities (UNFPA), 1979, Tanzania: *Report of Mission on Needs Assessment for Population Assistance*. New York.

United Republic of Tanzania (URT), March 1992, National Population Policy. Dar es Salaam: President's Office, The Planning Commission.

Urassa, E.J.N. et al., 1994, *Maternal Mortality in Dar es Salaam, Tanzania*. Manuscript submitted for publication.

Urassa, E.J.N., Kawo, G. et al., 1993, *Asphyxia Neotorum in Muhimbili Medical Centre*. Manuscript submitted for publication.

WHO, 1992, *Maternal mortality, a global fact book*.

2. The pubescent girl – past and present

Rita Liljeström, Patrick Masanja, Cletus P.B. Mkai,
and Zubeida Tumbo-Masabo

We are uncertain and hesitant about looking into the past. Do we fear entering exotic and imaginary societies that exist nowhere else but in the discourses of the cultural anthropologists? Hardly. One might have the impression that educated Tanzanians are shy and embarrased about their cultural roots. In fact, they have lost touch with them because of the degradation their societies experienced during the colonial era. In addition, public comments on ethnicity are generally avoided. In the name of national unity the topic is taboo. Accordingly, educated people appear to know little about their cultural past. Yet in private discussions, people often refer to their ethnic origins.

Customary patterns can still be traced in rural regions, as well as in many of the attitudes of the common people. It would be naive to believe that the marked differences between African and Eurasian family systems do not count. They do. They affect the way we Africans and Europeans, for instance, perceive marriage and parenthood. They cause us to hold different assumptions without being aware of these differences. The dialogue between us tends to become biased and be based on misunderstanding. The embarrassment of locals and lack of knowledge of foreigners make for a bad match.

On the other hand, the age-groups under twenty years make up more than half the nation's population. They are influenced by many forces other than tradition. We should avoid attributing motives and measures to the young that were appropriate to their ancestors but that are not so relevant to them. Somehow, we balance on the edge of continuity and change while trying to grasp at the reality of teenage girls.

Changing family patterns

By the beginning of this century, a number of social changes had taken root which had affected the family in many Tanzanian communities. Among the key processes were the pressures of labour migration and cash-crop agriculture which evolved during the colonial period. Male migration to the sisal plantations, mines or the coast began to affect communities, especially in the labour-exporting areas of southern and western Tanzania. In the cash-crop areas, the impact on families was felt in a rather different manner. What has taken place since independence in 1961 is the growing intensity of the process of social change. Other factors which have shaped the family, its structure, composition and functions, are rural migration, urbanization and formal education.

Tanzania has a variety of up to 120 communities with particular cultural practices as regards marriage and the family. These ethnic variations easily get lost in large-scale surveys. Aggregated national data tend to create the appearance of homogeneity by levelling out regional diversity. Wanting to avoid this semblance of uniformity, we have aimed at bearing witness to the vast differences in the communities where Tanzanian girls grow up to womanhood, and where they face the contradictory claims of an imported "civilization" and the remnants of tribal culture. Curious about traditional methods of fertility regulation, Mary Ntukula has focused on initiation rites (see Chapter 5 below), and the door to the African symbols and values regarding procreation was opened. Similarly, the focus in the case of the Mwera of Lindi (see Chapter 6) is on the role of initiation rites in a matrilineal tribe. These rites highlight the differences between matri- and patrilineal tribes.

In terms of affiliation, authority and inheritance, there are two types of families in Tanzanian communities, the patrilineal and the matrilineal. Thus, filiation, i.e., the status of sons and daughters, can either be established on the mother's or the father's side. In the former, filiation is mediated through the sisters and daughters of the men. The mother's brother has the authority over the children of his sister and they inherit through him. Patrilineal societies are based on the more familiar father – son relationship. Inheritance goes through the father. Nevertheless, there is no real symmetry. While "patriliny

Tanzania has more than 120 communities, each with their particular cultural practices as regards marriage and the family.
Photo: Charlotte Thege, Bazaar Bildbyrå, Stockholm

creates ties between the "father" and his wife's son, matriliny is not established between a mother and her daughters, but between the mother's brother and her children" (Meillassoux, 1981:23). Although the filiation is not symmetrical in terms of gender, generally the women in matrilineal societies are free from oppressive control and their husbands have less authority over them (Dube, 1993).

The situation is changing among, for example, the Zaramo, Luguru and other matrilineal communities in Tanzania. The patrilineal form of inheritance is gaining ground, especially among urban working families.

Despite various local differences, the family in many communities in Tanzania at the time of independence was extended, in contrast to the more nuclear type, particularly in the rural areas. Among the Sukuma of Mwanza and Shinyanga regions, for example, the *kaya* (family) not only included the head of the family, *namgi* (paterfamilias), his wife or wives, and her or their young children, but also grown-up children with their wives and children. Grown-up sons continued to stay in their father's household even when they got married. They belonged to his family and were under his paternal authority until the old man gave them permission to start their own separate units. This "traditional" form of family unit was progressively eroded during this century. Among the formally educated Sukuma and the migrant labourers who chose urban life, the extended type of family has increasingly given way to the nuclear family. However, among those who are engaged in agriculture and animal husbandry in the rural areas, remnants of the "traditional" family can still be seen. This is especially true of cattle herders, for even among the more sedentary cotton farmers the process of family change can be observed. However, members of extended families continue to support and assist each other even in the urban areas.

Bridewealth, a circulating pool of resources

The family as a social unit used to be constituted through a marriage in which some form of transaction took place from the husband's to the wife's family. The bridewealth, or *mahari*, traditionally took different forms. For some communities it took the form of labour. Among the Sukuma and Nyamwezi a newly married husband would stay with his in-laws for a year or two doing farm work if his family did not pay the required livestock as *nsabo* (bridewealth). Other communities used cattle or goods such as clothing, salt, etc., for the marriage transaction.

By studying the nature of property relations between husband and wife/wives and their parents, we can expose distinctive features of marriage in sub-Saharan Africa (Goody and Tambiah, 1973). Bridewealth is the commonest form of marriage transaction in Africa. It passes from the kin of the groom to those of the bride. It forms a societal fund, a circulating pool of resources, the movement of which corresponds to movements of rights over spouses, usually women.

Basically, bridewealth consists of a circulating pool of resources, since "it goes to the bride's male kin (typically brothers) in order that they can themselves take wives. Indeed it involves a kind of rationing system. What goes out for a bride has to come in for a sister" (Goody and Tambiah, 1973:5). A father has to ensure that the bridewealth he gets for a daughter will suffice to get him a daughter-in-law. Thus, a man is dependent "upon 'sisters' for bringing the wealth and 'fathers' for distributing it. This circulation tends to reinforce the authority of the father and emphasize the tie with the sister" (Goody and Tambiah, 1973:5).

Where the bridewealth is substantial, the marriage of girls tends to be early, and the men's late, since her marriage increases the father's wealth, while the son's diminishes it. The pressure on women to marry early is revealed in Grace Puja's and Rosalia Katapa's chapters below on pregnacy at school and arranged marriages. In fact, the different marriage ages of women and men have made African polygamy possible: "Bridewealth and polygyny play into each other's hands" (Goody and Tambiah, 1973:11). Katapa's study on arranged marriages among the Wakurya also has something to say about age differences at marriage.

In a general sense, the relative size of the payment is linked to the number of rights transferred. Where the rights in a woman's procreative power remain in her lineage, as in matrilineal societies, less bridewealth is given. Mary Shuma's chapter below on the Mwera of Lindi illustrates this point, also showing the associated high frequency of divorce. In matrilineal societies bridewealth is small and symbolic. It does not secure male filiation, but gives the husband exclusive sexual rights as long as the marriage persists. He has the right to demand compensation if this exclusiveness is violated. On the other hand, as Goody (1973) states, when we reach a bridewealth of twenty head of cattle or their equivalent "marriage becomes almost undissolvable" (Goody and Tambiah, 1973:4), since the bridewealth usually has to be repaid in the event of divorce. The wife's immediate kin will pressure her to remain with her husband or enter into a new marriage, in order to avoid such a repayment.

What role does bridewealth then play? Goody (1973) identifies the following functions:
– It secures the affiliation of the child to its father's kin group
– The question of affiliation is tied to inheritance and responsibility for bridewealth payments
– Non-bridewealth marriage means less conjugal control, more control of the bride by her own kin, and is hence associated with

less enduring marriages and less compensation in the case of adultery.

The different social destinations of the offspring also imply that pubescent adolescents are mobile in two ways. Where women stay in their original communities, to which men are invited to come to procreate and eventually live, the renewal of the group rests entirely on the reproductive capacities of the women born within the group. In the other case, where women move to their husband's group, reproduction depends on the political capacities of the communities to negotiate an adequate number of women (Meillassoux, 1981).

Comparing bridewealth to dowry

In considering bridewealth in a wider social context, Goody notes that inheritance in Africa usually is homogeneous by gender, i.e., males inherit from males, females from females. The variance in landholding was traditionally small compared to Europe and Asia. In economic terms, bridewealth has a levelling effect. In Africa, the land is often inherited within a lineage or clan. We can specify a certain tract of land as "belonging" to a particular group, whether it was matri- or patrilineal. The same applies to other property when the system of inheritance is harmonious with the system of descent. The members of the group will constitute a chain of potential heirs. All these features differ from the Eurasian dowry system.

Dowry is a part of a familial or conjugal fund, which passes down from holder to heir, and usually from the parents to the daughter. It is thus part and parcel of the transfer of familial property, but a process of transfer that includes women as well as men; that is male property is transmitted to women as full heir, semi-heirs or residual heirs (Goody and Tambiah, 1973:17).

In this system, the woman is not so much incorporated into her husband's lineage, but instead the bond between wife and husband is emphasized. While in Europe, for instance, the couple used to constitute a unit of common interest, in Africa the economic activities of husband and wife are typically distinct, even when there is no plural marriage. Not only is the bond between husband and wife/wives emphasized, but also the brother-in-law relationships. These are the men who have established an alliance around the wife, sister and daughter.

It has been argued that there are important differences between female inheritance and dowry, since they serve different purposes. While inheritance is *merely* a reflection of the general *descent ideology*, dowry is the result of a bargain and has a specific intention: that of linking the daughter – hence the family – with a particularly desirable son-in-law. According to Goody (1973), both of them reflect the interest in preserving the status of daughters as well as sons.

When there was a wide differentiation in landholding, it became a strategy of the utmost importance to preserve those differences for one's offspring. A girl's marriage tends to be made within the particular social group to which she belongs, in order to preserve her status and the family investments in it. An indication of this concern with the marriage of daughters, is the control exercised over their virginity. Dowry systems put emphasis on the downward transmission of property, upon the preference for children as against siblings.

...the distribution of bridewealth and dowry is consistent with differences in the openness of marriage. Closed systems tend to occur where property is differentiated; equally, open systems tend to be found where property is more evenly distributed. In-marriage is a policy of isolation; out-marriage involves wider exchanges, or interchanges, and it also involves levelling off, since it is a form of redistribution. Consequently, in-marriage tends to be associated with the complex stratification of Eurasia, out-marriage with the simpler stratification of African states where marriage alliances of the ruling estate are usually diversified between the different groups of society (Goody and Tambiah, 1973:32).

The authority of the old men

Some basic relationships in marriage thus differ between the bridewealth and dowry systems. According to Meillaussoux (1981), negotiations over marriage were the origin of politics and the source of elderly men's power. The authority of the older generation depends on the extent to which the young are dependent on them for bridewealth, cattle or cash or whatever. In some societies, the father can spend the bridewealth of his daughter to take himself another wife, while his sons have to delay their own marriages. However, nowadays a son can migrate to town in order to earn his bridewealth, just as a daughter can free herself from the marriage bond by selling sex in the towns.

With the increasing use of cash, *mahari* began to be paid in money, often moderate sums. The development of cash-cropping and the spread of the market economy has led to the payment of enormous sums of money amounting to thousands of Tanzanian shillings, or several head of cattle, depending on the wealth of the locality concerned.

Polygamy

There are monogamous and polygamous families. This depends on religious affiliation and economic capacity. The *Marriage Act* of 1971 in Tanzania, grants legal recognition to both types of marriage. Omari (1989) estimates that about 30 per cent of marriages in Tanzania are polygamous. Based on this observation, Omari concludes that, with increasing education among women, polygamous marriages will decrease, even among those whose religious practices allow them.

There are also indications that polygamy increases with women's age. However, it is evident that a significant number of currently married women, aged from fifteen to nineteen years are in polygamous marriages, i.e., 17 per cent.

Table 9. *Percentage distribution of all currently married women by age and number of co-wives*

| Number of co-wives | Age-group | | | | | |
	15–19	20–24	25–29	30–39	40–49	50+
None	82.7	79.1	75.3	69.5	58.9	68.0
One	13.8	16.6	19.4	22.2	23.1	21.2
Two	2.3	3.0	3.7	5.7	6.7	6.7
3–7	1.2	1.3	1.6	2.6	3.3	3.5
Total	100	100	100	100	100	100
Married in polygamous unions (per cent)	17.1	21.0	24.8	30.6	33.2	31.4

Sources: Bureau of Statistics, Ministry of Finance and Economic Planning, National Demographic Sample Survey of Tanzania (1973), Vol. II, table 2110

It is generally accepted that rural families in a "traditional setting" tend to have many children as a form of insurance. This is often due to relatively high death rates among children under five years of age due to the appalling state of the health services.

This situation may be in the process of transformation. In urban areas, employed mothers may have a smaller number of children than other families do. This is only from personal observation. Women and men in rural areas tend to marry at an earlier age, while those in urban areas, especially the employed, marry later.

School and work

The "traditional" family was in many communities the basic unit of production, consumption and socialization. These functions have been transformed, particularly in the urban setting. With the development of a new system of production based on cash crops, or market production rather than household consumption, the rural family on agricultural smallholdings retains its function as a unit of production in many communities. In the urban setting, however, with the diversity of occupations, household members are involved in a variety of jobs. Often parents and children may not be in the same occupation, and, except for traders, members of a family may be engaged in different sectors. Even in the rural areas, the growth of formal schooling has meant that the involvement of children in family economic activities is limited. While children in the rural setting may contribute to the family's economic activities when they are still in primary school, school children in the urban setting are mainly consumers. This statement needs to be qualified since among low-income groups, children may be engaged in petty trade.

By the time the child has reached the age of seven, the school system plays an increasingly important role in socialization. Tuli Kassimoto and Grace Puja describe the educational system and the involvement of girls in education and pregnancy at school elsewhere in this book. However, the prevailing poverty has struck many schools and demoralized teachers as well as pupils. Priscilla Olekambainei from the Ministry of Education shared with us her personal opinions (1990):
– The classes are too large
– Teachers often do not have enough teaching materials
– Teaching becomes dominated by rote learning or lectures
– Pupils quit school to do something more useful and interesting
– Teachers' salaries are not paid on time. Some teachers resort to
   small private projects which divert their attention from their
   teaching duties. In some periods nothing is taught
– Teachers often resort to using the cane for punishment
– There are schools where desks, good blackboards and windows
   are missing
– Most schools have no feeding programmes and some children
   have not eaten in the mornings
– Sometimes parents cannot raise money for fees, school
   uniforms and necessary materials
– Smoking, drinking and drugs are becoming a growing problem

Standard 7 pupils of Mwananyamala Primary School in Dar es Salaam.
Like many of their fellow pupils throughout the country, they took the
examination in 1990 sitting on the floor. The campaign launched by
President Mwinvi to find desks and chairs still has a long way to go.
Photo: Hilary Bujiku, Tanzania School of Journalism, Dar es Salaam

among the young. While smoking of bhangi and cigarettes is
found across the board among the youth, drinking of alcohol and
drug abuse is found mostly among youth from affluent and
bourgeois families.

According to Olekambainei, upbringing has become com-
partmentalized. Schools perform their duties as schools, parents do
what they can on their own, yet there is no bridge joining them.
Instead, the school and the home tend to operate as opposing camps.

What else is there for the school-leavers to do? What are their
options after they have dropped out or finished their primary
education? The 1990 Labour Force Survey shows that among the
employed, hourly underemployment rates are lower for teenage
girls than for teenage boys. Furthermore, underemployment rates
for teenage girls are lower than for most other female groups, except
the elderly. Employed teenage girls devote more person hours to
work than the rest of the population. Nevertheless, the current

unemployment rate is higher for teenage girls than for other female age-groups.

The majority of teenagers currently employed are in private trading, agriculture and the informal sector. More teenage girls than boys are employed by the government. However, more teenage boys are in other private jobs.

The Informal Sector Survey (ISS)[1] shows that the majority of teenagers are involved in trade and the restaurant business. For the ten to fourteen year old boys and girls involved in the informal sector, only about 8 per cent are paid employees, the rest are unpaid, probably family helpers. Proportionately more girls than boys are helpers rather than paid employees. Moreover, on average girls are paid less than boys for employment in the informal sector.

Table 10. *Average monthly earnings of paid employees in the informal sector by selected age-groups by sex*

| Age-group | Sex | | Total |
| | Male | Female | |
	Tshs	Tshs	
10–14	3,474	2,412	3,419
15–19	3,270	2,536	3,125

Source: Tanzania, The Informal Sector Survey (1991), Table EMP 11

Girls who are without meaningful employment or participation in income-generating activities, or who are receiving comparatively less renumeration when in work, are generally more prone to early sexual activity and pregnancy.

---

1. In Tanzania, the Informal Sector Survey (1991), agriculture was viewed differently depending on whether it was in an urban or a rural area. In rural areas, it was taken to be in the formal sector while in urban areas it was classified as part of the informal sector.

"Children of the bush"

Did there exist any "unwanted children" in the past? How did tribal societies treat unmarried mothers? There are four circumstances that dictated the African attitude to an "unwanted" child in the past: polygamy, the extended family, the material value of the child, and the prevalent love for children (Ndisi, 1964).

A man was forbidden to have sexual intercourse with his wife after she had given birth to a child. This prohibition may have continued for about two years. Polygamy made it possible for the man to adhere to this stringent rule. In this way, spacing was part of African customary practice. The health of a mother was not overtaxed and she could give the children all the care they needed.

In an extended family a child has many uncles, aunts and cousins. They are in much closer personal contact than the corresponding relatives are in Europe. A child without a mother or father was still very much wanted. Child adoption, in the European sense, was almost unknown. The need did not exist.

Great value was placed on even a female child. She was valued for the expected bridewealth she would bring to the parents, and the work she would do in the fields. Daughters, as well as sons, were also a kind of old age security for the parents. People in Africa love children. While violations of sexual rules were discouraged and punished, no social stigma was attached to the children of such liaisons. According to Ndisi, the value of the child is recognized irrespective of any sanctions against the mother.

Remember, in the past the ultimate object of marriage was not a wife but her progeny. In fact, the bride lost part of her identity in the matrimonial alliance. She was not chosen because of her own qualities but as part of a network of alliances, of previous obligations that her community had entered into, and because of the stage in the matrimonial cycle to which her age corresponded (Meillassoux, 1981). In patrilineal societies, the wife's children were incorporated into the husband's group.

...every marriage is an incorporation of "unrelated strangers" into "related strangers". Thus, the daughter of strangers has to be transformed into a childbearing wife. (Brandström, 1990:179)

Among the Sukuma-Nyamwezi, this transformation was narrated in terms of domestication of wild, unrelated female fertility:

While the woman, as wife, is likened to the sorghum field, ilale, which is wild bush and forest transformed into cultivated land, the woman outside the marital control of a man is wilderness, ipolu. To look for a wife is to go in search of arable land, kukoba malale.

...The domestication of "wild", unrelated female fertility is a prerequisite for the creation and continuation of the ordered cultural world budugu. Female fertility outside this order is "wild"; it belongs to the bush. Children born without a socially recognized father are literally called "children of the grass" or "children of the bush". This is not to say that these children are necessarily socially devalued, while they are anomalous in the sense that they are "one-sided" children, because, while lacking recognized agnatic identity, buta, they are associated only with their mother's side, migongo. (Brandström, 1990:179)

Because children by nature are so closely linked to their mothers, ideology is needed in order to suppress matrilineal descent. Hence, the rule is that descent can only be established through bridewealth payment. Therefore, a man's illegitimate children do not count as descendants. (Håkansson, 1991:191)

Playing down the maternal line also means, that although men desire to be the biological fathers of their wives' children, being a biological father as such does not make a man an ancestor; only the transfer of cattle will do that. For example, in Gusii thought, biological fatherhood is not necessary for establishment of descent. Children who are not biological are believed to inherit the characteristics from their legal father and his ancestors. (Håkansson, 1991:197)

No doubt, there have been variations in the ways different ethnic groups have reacted to unmarried mothers and their children. The glimpses given above have a certain congruence with the aims of the marriage; paternal rights are given more significance than biological fatherhood. Yet it is also true that "the child of the bush", who is not linked to any paternal line, is placed in the wilderness, outside the order, at least in a symbolic sense.

Abandoned young mothers

The family situation in the early 1960s was already deteriorating (Ndisi, 1965). The spread of monogamy and education have had bad side-effects in terms of unspaced families, maternal weariness, and neglected children. Monogamy, if not practised with some sense of personal discipline, can mean tragedy.

Education has alienated some of the youths from the old ways of life. No matter how superficial their education has been, it has led them to believe that they are superior and, therefore, to look down upon life in the villages. Besides, many of the old people are bewildered by "the hurricanes of change which have swept the countries in the last fifty years, and lost themselves, being unable to help and guide the young" (Ndisi, 1964).

The family's socialization role, especially in matters of fertility and sexuality, has become more uncertain. In some communities, initiation rituals were carried out for girls and boys at puberty, leading to circumcision. But in many cases, children reach this age when at school and the initiation ritual is often disrupted, or families cannot arrange for the initiation at the appropriate times. In many communities the grandparents educated children in matters of sexuality and fertility. Nowadays, the children often have moved away from the place where their grandparents stay. Several of our studies show how past intergenerational interventions have given way to bewilderment and lack of trust between the generations.

On the basis of her statistics on schoolgirl pregnancies, Priscilla Olekambainei tentatively concludes that many pregnant girls come from regions where strong traditions of indigenous "family-life education" have now been abandoned. Today, the young are left on their own to find out the facts of life by trial and error. In the process, many of them get trapped. Zubeida Tumbo-Masabo's chapter below underlines the need for instruction on sexuality and reproduction issues. What is offered now is *too little* and comes *too late*.

An emerging trend is the existence of single-parent families where widowed wives with children have to run the home. In urban areas, the phenomenon of unmarried working mothers also represents a growing trend in family life. Omari (1989) considers this as one of the most alarming situations in modern Tanzania.

The 1988 Population Census shows that nearly one out of three households is headed by a woman.

Table 11. *Female headed households*

Mainland Tanzania	29.9 per cent	4,297,407
Zanzibar	32.6 per cent	136,875
Whole country	30.0 per cent	4,419,914

Source: 1988 Population Census, table 24

Olekambainei highlights the unpromising prospects faced by the unmarried teenage mother. Expelled from school, she counts as uneducated and ends up jobless. Her options are few. She might make her living as a bar attendant or a housegirl, two occupations in which girls are often subjected to sexual harassment. Their children risk diseases related to malnutrition and poverty. In an effort to make ends meet, the women might exchange sexual favours for cash and other gifts. This exposes them to the considerable risk of contracting sexually transmitted diseases, not least AIDS. The role of the boyfriends' gifts emerges in what Betty Komba-Malekele and Rita Liljeström write below about looking for men.

Societies all around the world have sacrificed their daughters as warning examples to others, in defence of virginity, a good match, advantageous bridewealth negotiations, all to honour the man's control of the woman's capacity to generate life. In such cases, where are the mothers who witness the trauma that their daughters experience?

With whom do the mothers side?

It has been argued (Fox, 1980; Ariés, 1962) that pre-industrial societies, by and large, consisted of three blocs of people. One dividing line lay between men and women, and the other separated older men from younger men. Among the women there was no dividing line, since only married women, only women who had proved themselves as mothers, mattered. They formed the third bloc, the collective of women. Hence, the structure of gender and age is asymmetrical; there is the young men's collective as well as that of the elderly men. The point to be made here is the absence of young women as a group in their own right. Their presence is loose and transitional. Soon they will be married off, and eventually, as mothers, they will enter the women's bloc.

Nancy Foner (1984) has studied ages in conflict in non-industrial societies. However, conflicts often mean that two parties join against a third. For example, the mothers of the community enter into a coalition with the generation of their husbands and brothers, the elderly men, to maintain control of the young. Or the mothers ally themselves with the young generation, especially with their sons, in common opposition to the elderly men.

There is one more option; all the men come together to maintain control over the women. While the young men are aware that, one day, they will succeed the older men and in their turn uphold the privileges of age and of the male gender, the age relationship between women has no such promise. In fact, the older and younger women's interests are so far apart that the two groups seldom support each other. Hence, the young women do not exist as a collectivity in their own right. The old men negotiate their marriages, the young men get wives in return for their sisters' bridewealth, the young women are strangers to be domesticated and incorporated into their husbands' family line. The elderly women, the mothers-in-law, tend to side with their sons.

But what about a daughter's own mother? Do not the mothers protect and support their daughters? To some extent, but there are limits. If a daughter misbehaves, the blame is put on the mother and affects the good reputation of the whole family. Therefore, the mothers may detach themselves from the needs of their daughters.

This is illustrated in the chapter on adolescent mothers by Alice Rugumyamheto, Virginia Kainamula and Juliana Mziray below. The pregnant girls' fear of their parents' reaction reveals a lack of mutual trust.

Magdalena Kamugisha Rwebangira poses the question, what has the law got to do with it? elsewhere in this volume. She looks at the law from a woman's perspective and bears witness to the concealment and desperation that lead unmarried mothers to the courts.

Approaching teenage girls

We have begun to move closer to her, the teenage girl, passing through much of what other sources tell us about her. We have compiled statistics, although not much data are available. We have identified demographic and reproductive health policies that are focused on teenage girls. We have looked at the pubescent girl's position in tribal cultures of the past. We are forcibly struck by the realization that she is socially constructed to fit the aims of other people. Everywhere, including in our studies, the girl on the threshold of womanhood appears as she is seen by others, be it with sympathy, slander or condemnation. We wanted to make the teenage girl herself heard. However, that is not an easy task and so far we have barely glimpsed her, being ourselves entangled in all that is attributed to her, and probably also in our suppressed memories of our own confused youth.

References

Ariés, Philippe, 1962, *Centuries of Childhood*. London: Penguin Books.

Brandström, Per, 1990, "Seeds and Soil: The Quest for Life and the Domestication of Fertility in Sukuma-Nyamwezi Thought and Reality", in Anita Jacobson-Widding and Walter van Beek (eds.), *The creative Communion. Studies in Cultural Anthropology*. Uppsala: Almqvist & Wiksell International.

Bureau of Statistics, 1992, *1988 Population Census, National profile.* Dar es Salaam: Planning Commission.

Dube, Leela, 1993, "Who Gains from Matriliny? Men, Women and Change in a Lakshadweep Island". Paper presented at conference on Changing Gender and Kinship in sub-Saharan Africa and South Asia, University of Nairobi.

Foner, Nancy, 1984, *Ages in Conflict, a cross-cultural perspective on inequality between old and young.* New York: Columbia University Press.

Fox, Robin, 1980, *The Red Lamp of Incest.* London: Hutchinson.

Goody, Jack and S.J. Tambiah, 1973, *Bridewealth and Dowry.* Cambridge: Cambridge University Press.

Håkansson, Thomas, 1991, "Descent and Sex among the Gusii", in Jacobson-Widding and van Beek, op. cit.

Meillassoux, Claude, 1981, *Maidens, Meal and Money.* Cambridge: Cambridge University Press.

National Informal Sector Survey, 1991, Tabulations Table EMPII.

Ndisi, M.A.O., 1965, "The Unwanted Child, African Pattern", in *Sex and Human relations.* Proceedings of the Fourth Conference of the region for Europe, Near East and Africa. IPPF, Excerpta Medica Foundation.

Olekambainei, P., 1990, *Paper prepared for the training workshop for The Teenage Girls and their Reproductive Health project.* University of Dar es Salaam.

Omari, C.K., 1989, *The Emerging Family Structure in Tanzania and the Work of the Church*, in Mimeo, Department of Sociology, University of Dar es Salaam.

3. Girls in education and pregnancy at school

Grace Khwaya Puja and Tuli Kassimoto

There are two educational systems which operate in Tanzania, one on the mainland and the other in Zanzibar. In mainland Tanzania, primary education, standards 1 to 7, was made universal in 1977. In Zanzibar, primary and lower secondary schooling is free and compulsory in terms of the *Education Act* of 1982. Primary education is from standard 1 to 8 and lower/junior secondary is from terms 1 to 3. In both systems of education students sit for the same Form 4 school certificate examination. Higher and tertiary education are provided by the Union government.

The present chapter deals with the educational opportunities that are available to girls in Tanzania. Tuli Kassimoto writes about the situation in mainland Tanzania, while Grace Khwaya Puja dwells on conditions on the island of Zanzibar. Grace Puja also reports on her study of pregnancies among secondary school girls. Here, she gives accounts of her interviews with school girls who have been pregnant, their parents, teachers and headmistresses, and also the educational authorities.

Education for girls in mainland Tanzania

The education system consists of seven years of primary education, four years of lower secondary education, two years of higher secondary education, and three, four or five years of university education depending on the course taken. Primary education is compulsory and universal. Children generally start primary education at the age of seven. In 1991, 75 per cent of the population in the age group from seven to thirteen years were enroled in primary schools. Primary education is terminal for most students.

At the end of primary education, pupils sit for the Standard 7 primary school leaving examination (PSLE). Only those meeting specially designed criteria are selected to go on to public secondary schools. In 1991, these candidates constituted only 5 per cent of all primary-school leavers. This meant that 95 per cent of primary-school leavers did not continue with school education. Girls constituted only 43 per cent of the total Form 1 students. Others who could afford to pay for secondary education enroled in private secondary schools. Girls were at a disadvantage, in that some parents preferred to send their sons rather than their daughters to private secondary schools (Katunzi et al, 1991). In 1991, 46.7 per cent of the total students who enroled at private secondary schools were girls. The primary school leaving examination has had a retarding effect on the schooling process because of the low proportion of pupils entering secondary schools and the lack of alternative opportunities for primary-school leavers. A majority of the girls end up either getting married or falling pregnant at an early age.

As already mentioned, secondary education is of two types, lower secondary education is for four years, forms 1 to 4, and higher education is for two years, forms 5 to 6. Upon completion of lower secondary education, students take the Form 4 national examination. Depending on the vacancies available, those who pass this examination well are enroled in Form 5. The others join tertiary institutions like teacher education, nursing, full technician certificate courses and so on.

After two years of study, those who go into secondary education sit for the Form 6 examinations. Those who pass well enrol at institutions of higher learning such as the university, or they enrol at professional institutions such as the Institute of Finance Management, Institute of Development Management, etc.

Enrolment

The Universal Primary Education (UPE) policy was initiated in 1977. UPE was a positive development for women. Full equality of access to primary schooling was achieved. For example, in 1986 enrolment of girls in primary schools was 50 per cent and in 1991 it was 49 per cent. Though enrolment has been equalized, there is the continuing problem of a high drop-out rate at the primary school level. Many girls do not complete seven years of primary education, an important element in uplifting the status of women. The drop-out rate and the reasons for dropping out are indicated in the following table.

Table 12. *Drop-outs at primary school and reasons for dropping out*

| Reasons | | Years | | | | |
| | | 1990 | | | 1991 | |
	girls	boys	total	girls	boys	total
Truancy	19,115	24,585	43,700	16,401	20,540	36,941
Pregnancy	1,687	-	1,687	2,946	-	2,946
Death	1,114	1,415	2,529	1,317	1,600	2,917
Others	2,037	2,211	4,248	1,234	1,419	2,653
Total	23,953	28,211	52,164	21,898	23,559	43,957

Source: Ministry of Education (1990 and 1991)

It can be noted from Table 12 that more boys drop out from primary education than girls. Boys drop out mainly by way of truancy. Some of the boys who drop out become involved in petty businesses, some herd cattle and some move to urban areas to seek employment. Hence, boys engage in productive activities, whereas girls who drop out because of pregnancy, get married. In some cases, girls drop out from school because of pregnancy but are recorded as truants. Other girls are truants and drop out because they are needed to perform household chores. They finally end up marrying at an early age. The majority of primary school pupils enrol at the age of seven years and complete Standard 7 by the age of thirteen. In 1991, more than 85 per cent of the students who completed Standard 7 were between thirteen and sixteen years. This means that those who drop out from primary schools are between seven and thirteen years of age. These girls are the teenage mothers who face health problems during pregnancy and delivery.

The law on universal primary education made enrolment and attendance at school compulsory. Parents who failed to comply with this regulation were fined. This is a progressive system as far as girls' education is concerned. But some parents who do not want to enrol their children in school have managed to avoid being fined. For example, some deceive the school authorities by telling them that they intend to transfer their daughter to another school. Once they get the transfer certificate, they do not register their daughter in any school and may force her to get married at an early age. Although the law enforces attendance, the root socio-economic factors affecting girls' educational access, attributed social status and social conduct remain untouched (Mbilinyi *et al.*, 1991).

More females enrol in private than in public secondary schools. The enrolment in 1990 in Form 1 in public secondary schools was 39.2 per cent of total enrolment while in private secondary schools it was 46.7 per cent. In Form 5, enrolment in 1990 in public secondary schools was 18.3 per cent while in private secondary schools it was 23.2 per cent. This means that girls depend more on the private sector for secondary schooling. This has repercussions for their performance at the higher education level since secondary education opens the doors to higher and tertiary education. Fewer girls in secondary education means fewer women in higher education. Table 13 indicates this trend.

Table 13. *Women's enrolment as percentage of total enrolment*

| Educational level | Years | | | | |
	1987	1988	1989	1990	1991
Std 1–7	49.8	49.7	49.6	49.5	49.4
Form 1					
–Public	37.6	40.4	41.8	39.2	43.2
–Private	45.5	47.3	46.1	46.7	46.7
Form 5	19.4	22.8	27.9	19.8	25.5
–Public	19.7	24.5	28.9	18.3	27.5
–Private	18.4	18.7	25.2	23.2	21.6
Teacher education	40.9	41.6	40.8	42.7	44.8
Technical colleges*	7.5	5.1	6.9	6.7	-
University education* (Undergraduate)	15.2	16.9	17.1	18.8	-

Source: Basic Education Statistics in Tanzania (1992)
* Statistics for 1991 for Technical colleges and University education were not available as they fell under a new Ministry of Higher Education and Technology.

The enrolment of women in post-secondary education, university and other tertiary institutions is extremely limited. Table 13 indicates that the percentage of women entering technical education is particularly small. In 1990, only 6.7 per cent of the total trainees who enrolled in technical education were women. The percentage of women decreases as the level of education increases. For example, in 1990, 39.2 per cent of students who entered public secondary schools were girls, but only 19.8 per cent of students entering Form 5 and 18.8 per cent of those enrolling for university education were girls.

The Curriculum

The structure and content of the curriculum in primary and secondary education are intended to equip students with the basic skills of a terminal education and critical thinking and analysis. In order to implement this curriculum, Education for Self Reliance (ESR) was developed. ESR was introduced with the aim of providing relevant, adaptive education. School-leavers were to go back to the land and become productive farmers.

However, those responsible for implementing ESR, that is the teachers, administrators and pupils, viewed formal education as the key to wage employment outside the rural areas. The structural context in which ESR was set was highly bureaucratic. The curriculum was centrally developed and teachers, administrators and pupils had no decision-making powers in regard to the curriculum. Freyhold (1977) and Sumra (1985) found that primary education lacked the practical content required for the ESR programme, e.g., there was no manual work, there was a shortage of equipment and materials and there were conflicts over the distribution and proceeds of ESR. Hence, Mbilinyi *et al.* (1991) assert that ESR has not been able to achieve its goals. Theory and practice remain unintegrated. National examinations and a national curriculum, coupled with students' and parents' expectations of further education, mean that the purpose of schooling has become to pass examinations.

Teaching materials continue to portray men and women in stereotyped roles, and the real contributions of women to society and the economy are not included in the texts. Subjects of particular

Pupils in a class-room performance
Daily News, Dar es Salaam

benefit to women, such as family-life education, are not taught. This has had adverse effects on girls' education, in that girls are not made aware of how their bodies function. Because they remain ignorant of this, they fall pregnant and drop out of school. The content of the curriculum is not used to transmit information of specific use and interest to girls.

It has been observed that teachers tend to favour boys unconsciously by paying more attention to them in the classroom (Mbilinyi *et al.*, 1991). Furthermore, schools have an authoritarian school management system in which corporal punishment is used. The teacher-centred pedagogy and the competitive basis of classroom dynamics combine to make an environment which is unfriendly to girls.

Academic Performance

The criteria used to evaluate school performance are the examination results taken at the end of Standard 7. It was observed that girls' performance was generally poorer in all subjects in the Primary

School Leaving Examination (PSLE) (Ndabi cited in TADREG, 1989). Moreover, differences in performance have been noted between schools. In all-girl schools and all-girl boarding schools, the girls had a very high achievement record compared to girls in co-education schools. The reasons for girls' lower performances vary. There are socio-economic factors, for example, girls have a heavier work burden at home. Another explanation is that the school culture is male-oriented and male-dominated, thus girls become victims.

Girls reaching adolescence face conflicting role-expectations and fear being labelled as "too smart" in school. At adolescence, girls think that to be female means not to be intelligent, ambitious and resourceful. Girls internalize these views of inferiority and lower intelligence. For example, many girls think that maths and sciences are subjects for males and believe that science subjects are more difficult than arts subjects. Consequently, they enrol in the arts rather than the sciences. The performance in the sciences in the Form 4 and 6 examinations are generally poor, hence girls opt out of the sciences (Mbilinyi *et al.*, 1992).

Low expectations of success probably encourage poor performance. The dynamics of teacher – student relations also affect girls' choices in respect to science subjects. In 1989, Sekwao found out that 90 per cent of the technical teachers, 81 per cent of maths and 66 per cent of science teachers were men, compared to only 42 per cent male arts teachers. This probably influences girls' education.

Girls' Education in Zanzibar

Colonial era

Historically, education in Zanzibar has had a dual character. Since the majority of inhabitants of Zanzibar have always been Moslems, Islamic education has always been regarded with great respect and the majority of parents saw no reason to change or adapt to a Western form of education.

There were other problems which were faced by the colonial government in providing education in Zanzibar. These were related to the various ethnic groups which lived in Zanzibar. Apart from Arabs, Africans, and Swahilis[1] there were people of Asian origin, Indians, Chinese, Japanese, Persians and Syrians. It was very difficult to cater for the educational needs of all these people.

The first modern schools were those built by Catholic missionaries and the education they provided was mainly religious until the government decided in the 1940s to incorporate Koranic schools into the government primary schools. This led to the removal of friction between school and village and Koran teachers brought their pupils with them and a Koran class was established as the foundation of each rural school. As a result, there were more enrolments and the Domestic Science school, opened in 1944, provided practical classes for girls in Zanzibar. Emphasis on girls' education was part of the Ten Year Development Plan between 1946 and 1955.

In Zanzibar, unlike in Tanganyika, girls dropped out of school not because of school fees (since education was free) but rather because of early marriage. Boys also dropped out of school but they did so in order to search for employment and because of the clove harvest. Consequently, education in Zanzibar made limited progress.

For instance, in 1952, a school in Pemba closed down due to lack of support. Of the total of 5,544 pupils in the predominantly male primary schools, there were only 410 girls (7.39 per cent). In isolated areas, girls were allowed to attend boys' schools if parents consented, although there were also girls-only schools.

Openings for girls were very limited because the only practical subjects taught to girls were domestic science and dress-making. Teacher training colleges provided opportunities for female students but marriage took preference over career in most cases and many Arab parents refused to allow their daughters to attend such

---

1. According to Furley and Twayson (1978), with the coming of missions to work among freed slaves, education in Zanzibar fell into distinct racial divisions: Arabs, Swahilis, Africans and the various Asian communities.
Furley also points out that intermarriage between Arabs and Africans resulted in the Swahili people, with their own language, Swahili, and culture. Originally Swahili meant "a man of the coast" (Furley, 1978:35, 28–9).

institutions, partly because they feared their daughters would be converted to Christianity (Furley, 1978:44).

Racial discrimination, especially against people of African origin, was another contributing factor in limiting girls' education in Zanzibar.

The 1964 revolution and after

The 1964 revolution was aimed at eliminating discrimination of any kind in all sectors of society. The new government started by declaring education free and non-racial. This led to more enrolments by African students. As a result, more girls attended school but they were often held back by their parents who insisted that girls should be married at puberty, i.e., around thirteen years of age. During this period, girls stay at home and prepare themselves for their role as wives and mothers. Therefore, female drop-out rates are more common after Standard 7. For example, in 1985, among the 4,172 girls who were in Standard 6, only 3,019 continued to Standard 7 (72.4 per cent), while 27.6 per cent dropped out of school (Mwanze, 1991).

Apart from changes involving enrolment figures, the number of schooling years changed from eight to eleven, which included three years of junior secondary education.

Girls' enrolment in primary and secondary schools

According to data from the Department of Statistics in Zanzibar, more girls than boys were enrolled in primary schools in 1989 (United Republic, 1992:65). However, as girls advance to the higher levels of education, their enrolment rates decrease. At the secondary level, the enrolment of girls has been consistently lower than that of boys. For example, between 1981 and 1990, girls' enrolment in secondary schools was less than that of boys. One of the major contributing factors is early marriage.

When girls reach puberty, at the age of twelve to sixteen years, many of them do not continue with education. According to Islam, which is the dominant religion of Zanzibar, girls should not be publicly exposed after puberty. Some elders, in fact, insist that exposed girls are not suitable for marriage. Therefore, many parents in Zanzibar do not allow their daughters to continue with education after puberty.

Girls' enrolment in tertiary and higher institutions of education

Girls' enrolment at the tertiary and higher educational levels decreases even more than at lower levels. In 1985, eighteen girls among the 216 who sat for the national Form 4 examination were selected for Form 5 and technical colleges (8.3 per cent). Although this number increased to 62 in 1990, this figure was only 31.4 per cent of the total number of girls who were in Form 4 the previous year (Mwanze, 1991:20, citing Zanzibar Ministry of Education, Budget Speech 1990–91). Besides, in 1981, girls represented 26 per cent of the total enrolment in teacher colleges.

Statistics on higher education show that girls' enrolment in various institutions of higher learning outside Zanzibar is either very low or non-existent. For example, in 1988, 41 per cent of Zanzibari first-year students at the University of Dar es Salaam and Sokoine were girls, but this decreased to 15 per cent in 1989–90. Besides, there were no girls at all represented at other institutions such as the Institute of Development Management (IDM), Institute of Finance Management (IFM), or the Cooperative College, Moshi (CCM).

Contributing to the small percentage of girls at higher levels of education is the fact that many of them either get married after reaching puberty (according to the Islamic marriage law) or fall pregnant before marriage.

Girls' school performance and subject combinations

At the end of Form 3, students take an examination, the results of which are used to select students for Form 4. It is at this level that many girls do not proceed further. For instance, in 1985 there were 2,131 girls in Form 3 but only 302 or 14.1 per cent of them were selected for Form 4. Girls' performance at the secondary school, as revealed by the number of girls selected for Form 4, has declined from 14.1 per cent in 1985 through 9.9 per cent in 1987 to 6.6 per cent in 1989.

Most girls prefer language subjects and very few, or none at all, study technical subjects because they do not like science subjects (Mwanze, 1991:31).

Tradition and girls' education

According to Mwanze (1991), in Zanzibar past and present, the girl's place was and is in the kitchen. As such, socialization by the family and at school emphasizes that girls should be submissive, subservient home-keepers and breeders. Hence, whatever a girl does, the key reference point is *"when you get married"*.

At school, girls are discouraged from studying science and mathematics because if a girl is very intelligent she might discourage a potential husband since many men fear clever women. Such women are seen as a threat and intelligence is believed to make women less feminine and less womanly. As a result, girls fear being labelled *"too smart at school"*.

Emphasis on marriage is reflected in the Zanzibar marriage law which allows girls at the age of eighteen and above to get married while they are still at school. However, those girls who do get married and continue at school face other problems. They are more likely to suffer emotional pressures from their spouses which may cause them to drop out of school. Very few girls are encouraged by their husbands to continue at school.

Pregnancy at school

The dismissal of secondary school pupils for pregnancy only affects girls (TADREG, 1990:3). However, the exact numbers are difficult to obtain mainly because many girls leave school before their pregnancy has been noticed and some may secretly abort. Besides, most girls from the economically well-off families may even have access to methods of modern contraception. Therefore, it is primarily girls from poor families who are expelled from school, basically because they are less well informed and cannot afford abortions.

The concerns that surround secondary school girls arise mainly from the role that these educated girls are expected to play in society and the fact they are among the 13 per cent or less of the total primary school graduates who are lucky enough to be selected for secondary education each year in Tanzania (Nyerere, 1967).

The few girls who are selected for secondary education form the only segment of the female population that at least has a possibility of participating in high-level manpower development. It is, therefore, quite a setback when such girls drop out because of pregnancy. Also, parents who have had to make sacrifices to invest in their daughters' education, sometimes feel disappointed.

My study was an attempt to look at factors that contribute to pregnancy among secondary school girls and to compare different regions. I decided to go to two coastal (Tanga and Pemba) and two up-country (Kilimanjaro and Mwanza) secondary schools. On the coast, the schools visited were for girls only, while the up-country schools were co-educational, and thus reflected cultural differences. I felt the need to compare regions in order to find out if they also differed in socio-economic and cultural characteristics, and consequently in values and practices relating to school-girl pregnancies.

I was able to identify fifteen secondary school girls who had been pregnant and who had personal experience of having been expelled from school because of their pregnancies. I interviewed them all as well as sixteen of their parents.

I also wanted to explore the attitudes of other pupils towards pregnant schoolmates by distributing a questionnaire to 200 secondary school students, 50 from each of the four schools. In addition, I interviewed teachers and headmistresses as well as ministerial officials in Dar es Salaam and Zanzibar.

Experiences of secondary school girls who had been pregnant

I felt it was important to look at the experiences of girls who had been expelled from school. According to the girls themselves, they became pregnant for three major reasons:

– They had been involved in a love relationship. They were simply attracted to the man
– Some of the girls became pregnant because they were economically dependent on the men who caused the pregnancy. They pointed out that they relied on these men for economic assistance because their parents were not adequately supporting them. One girl narrated how she travelled without enough money from Tanga all the way to Ifakara Agricultural Secondary School
– The third major reason given was peer-group influence. Several girls explained how their fellow girl-friends who had male company were better off economically and that this influenced their decision to have male friends. They also felt the need to be up-to-date and to move with the times like their friends.

It can be seen that while developmental changes at adolescence, the need to be loved, poverty at home, and peer-group influence are here to stay, there still exist strategies for advising girls on how to handle these pressures. Hence, we need to analyse how these issues can be handled with adequate and appropriate knowledge. Many girls simply face humiliation and misery.

Mwanahawa from Mwanza became pregnant because she and her boy-friend had been in love with each other for two years, but she did not expect to conceive. And when this happened, she was in Form 4 and was eighteen years old. This means that the friendship had begun when she was in Form 2 and sixteen.

After missing her period, she did not tell anybody until she was three-months pregnant, when she confided in her mother. Mwanahawa painfully narrated to me how her neighbours were treating her. They were talking about her and when I visited her, everybody was curious to know what was happening. At that time, the child was only two months old and, therefore, her feelings about her experience were still strong. She felt bad, her social status had been lowered, people gossiped about her; all this in addition to her expulsion from school.

Concerning her relationship with the man who impregnated her, Mwanahawa told me that he was willing to marry her and her parents had agreed to the marriage.

Things were not so bad for *Rachel* either. When I met her she lived in Tanga. Her mother was the second wife of a businessman with secondary education. The parents were not living together. When Rachel was expelled from school, she went to live with her mother.

According to Rachel, the reason for her becoming pregnant was basically economic. She was living with her stepsister, and her father only paid her school fees but she had to look after her own personal expenses. Her sister gave her food at home but nothing else. In these circumstances, she found a male friend who ultimately intended to marry her. This man supported her financially. She felt that becoming pregnant was unfortunate because the final goal of their relationship was marriage. At that time she was in Form 3.

Rachel was expelled from school and she was sick almost throughout the pregnancy. Now she aims to take care of her child and later complete her studies so that she can find employment. She wants to be independent.

Nuru was from Tanga. While in Form 2, she was very active in netball games. She used to travel to other areas to compete with students from other secondary schools. This was how she met Hamidu. They had not been friends for long, but they liked each other and had sexual relations which resulted in pregnancy. She recalls now that her relationship with Hamidu was mainly the result of peer-group influence, because basically she was a very shy and quiet girl.

Nuru did not know that she was pregnant even after missing her periods for four months. She was worried, but did not tell anybody.

Stella is a daughter of an illiterate peasant from Kilimanjaro rural area. Her mother makes her living in small business. The parents are separated. Stella was Paul's girl-friend for a long time before they became involved in the love affair which resulted in Stella's pregnancy. However, she indicates that Paul was not the first man she had had a love affair with. There was another man she had met briefly. When she was five-months pregnant, she told her mother about her condition. She had the very bitter experience of being driven away from home by her parents, and Paul categorically denied that he knew her. Her parents did not help her in any way.

When I asked these girls to mention any problems that they had faced at school as a result of being pregnant, they listed the following in order of severity:
– low social status and lack of respect
– shame
– isolation, people avoiding them
– disowned and driven away from home by parents
– denounced by the man responsible for the pregnancy.

These difficulties were in addition to the girls' inability to continue with their studies, expulsion from school, and the added burden of pregnancy and a child without any kind of economic support. For most of them, their future expectations were destroyed and they were psychologically disturbed and socially displaced and disadvantaged.

It is important to emphasize that at adolescence the question of social identity is crucial. Social identity includes how people seek self-respect and affirmation from others. Therefore, a pregnant girl who becomes isolated, despised by her peers, parents and teachers will definitely suffer an identity crisis, and she might commit or succumb to acts such as abortion, suicide, etc. Ordinary adolescents, especially those in rural areas, have no clear or unambiguous notion about what it means to realize oneself as woman, even when they have none of the problems associated with pregnancy. They face problems of how to handle standards of evaluation in their different personal relationships, especially with the opposite sex.

What do the parents say?

When I asked the parents about what they believed to be the reason for their daughter's pregnancy, they mentioned ignorance of sex, peer-group influence and economic problems. They saw ignorance as the main reason. Parents also seem to place more emphasis on peer-group influence than on the economic hardships that their daughters cited.

Parents were very bitter about what had happened to their daughters. A father even shed tears as he narrated the experience of his *Judica* who had fallen pregnant in Form 3. Judica's father blamed it on the influence of the peer-group.

From interviews with mothers and some fathers, I noted with much concern that it is the fathers who generally contribute most to the discomfort of the girls. For instance, in Kilimanjaro, I interviewed two fathers. Though they were both fairly well educated, they differed in the way they treated their pregnant daughters after they were expelled from school. While one of the fathers was sympathetic and understanding, the other had not seen his daughter, who was staying with her sister, since she was expelled from school more than a year earlier. He also showed how emotionally upset he was by the incident and argued that seeing his daughter and his grandchild might in fact make him collapse and die, because it was so painful to see his bright daughter discontinue her studies.

What do secondary school students think?

Some students think that girls like to have sexual relationships with wealthy men. Besides, even wealthy men themselves prefer to have sex with young girls. Students referred to these men as "sugar daddies" and to the young girls as "spring chickens". According to them these terms are well known.

Some students believe that school girls are seduced because they are not very knowledgeable about sex. Other students, especially those from Pemba, are convinced that adolescent girls are strongly attracted to men. This view was not supported by some students from Kilimanjaro who asserted that economic factors, such as receiving gifts or money, are the main issue.

Many Pemba students were also of the opinion that if the girls were seriously following their religion, they would not become pregnant at school. Premarital sex, according to Pemba students and some from the mainland schools, is one of the sins prohibited by the holy books of the Koran and the Bible. Other students, from both the mainland and Pemba, think that adherence to religion is not enough, since they have seen very faithful school girls become pregnant. Some also felt that foreign influences, especially foreign films, videos and magazines spoil the teenage girls.

I had given the students an open-ended question on how they would personally prevent a pregnancy either for themselves or for their girl-friends. I have summarized and translated the girls' and boys' responses separately.

The girls' ways of preventing pregnancy are as follows:
– avoid sexual act
– control desire for material things
– listen to elders' advice
– avoid friendships with boys and men
– concentrate on studies.

The above list seems to reflect elders' teachings rather than the girls' own convictions. Boys, on the other hand, have a list which seems to reflect their own thinking rather than that of their elders. However, they do not risk missing any periods and having no-one to confide in.

The boys would prevent pregnancy by the following means:
– use socks (condoms)
– avoid sexual act
– accomodate to their girl-friends' safe periods
– follow religious teachings and beliefs
– have sex less often.

The above list differs from that given by the girls. With the exception of the avoidance of the sexual act and following religious teachings, the remaining methods clearly show that boys are actively involved in premarital sex. The list also suggests that the boys are either more informed than girls, or the girls are too shy to tell the truth. This, of course, is exactly what is expected of girls. This poses a danger because boys will take the lead in demanding sex from girls who are either less knowledgeable or too shy to resist.

The reader is referred to the two different regional systems of education in Tanzania as regards primary and lower secondary school levels (the latter refers to Forms 1 to 3). In Zanzibar, primary education and lower secondary education is free and compulsory. Any girl who becomes pregnant while attending either of the two levels is prosecuted together with the man responsible for the pregnancy. If found guilty, they are both imprisoned for a period of not less than two years. However, most often the man denounces the girl and so she goes to prison alone.

In mainland Tanzania, the secondary school girl who becomes pregnant is expelled from school but is not taken to court. The man responsible is usually not bothered by the law but the girl's parents may try to make him accountable, although they will not often succeed.

It is within this framework that parents, teachers and officials suggested the following steps to be taken by the Ministry of Education:

1. The government, through the Ministry of Education in main-land Tanzania, should enact a law that will work in favour of pregnant secondary school girls. This law should ensure that men who impregnate secondary school girls are severely punished

2. Another suggestion was that the Ministry of Education should make such a provision in the law that men who cause pregnancies among secondary school girls should be made to refund all expenses incurred by parents in educating these girls.

This suggestion was made by fathers who were very bitter about the men who impregnated their daughters and then denounced them. Parents also made a strong appeal for the Ministry of Education to allow pregnant secondary school girls to continue with their studies after the birth of their children.

Teachers' and educational administrators' views

The teachers and educational administrators argued that the poor educational level and illiteracy of many parents indicated that they were not aware of the benefits of educating their daughters and instead tended to stress the value of marriage and child-bearing.

Moreover, the teachers stressed that foreign influences through the mass media play a role, since teenagers like to identify themselves with famous people such as pop singers and film stars. They tend to imitate any kind of fashions that appear to be popular among other teenagers.

The teachers referred to the fact that many families in Tanzania

Since parents and the state have invested heavily in young girls'
education, a schoolgirl's pregnancy is seen as a great loss.
Daily News, Dar es Salaam

are facing economic hardship. As such, girls from utterly poor families resort to friendships with rich men to alleviate their poverty. Parents are too busy to take care of their children and girls may become involved in heterosexual relationships without the knowledge of their parents.

The educational administration also saw the fact that many pupils have to travel long distances between home and school as a contributory factor. This exposed girls to the dangers of being raped or seduced by men.

A closer analysis of the Kilimanjaro and Pemba schools showed that they differed in two respects. While in Pemba, more than half the students who answered my questionnaire indicated that their mothers were illiterate, in Kilimanjaro only one out of six gave that answer. In Kilimanjaro a third of the pupil sample had well-educated mothers, while none of the Pemba pupils had. All the students that were involved in my study at the Pemba school are Moslems, while at Kilimanjaro 4 per cent are Moslems and the rest are Christians.

I assume that these differences have a bearing on my findings about factors that contribute to secondary school pregnancies. In

Kilimanjaro, the students in my sample seemed to emphasize economic reasons, while the Pemba students placed more weight on developmental aspects by emphasizing the need for girls to be married immediately after puberty. The differences might well reflect different views on sexuality.

According to a teacher at the Pemba school, girls from rural areas tend to marry earlier than those from urban areas. Most rural parents believe that girls should be married immediately after puberty. It is believed that sex is best when the girls are adolescents and that after that period they are "spoilt" and are no longer as sexually appealing for marriage.

Also, it is in the rural areas that parents are illiterate and poor and do not appreciate the value of educating girls. The teacher also argued that most parents in rural areas marry off their daughters because of poverty. They cannot afford to educate them. So marrying them off transfers the economic burden to the husband.

Besides, parents get a lot of bridewealth – especially in Zanzibar where many girls tend to marry either in Arab countries or in Pakistan and the bridewealth is paid in foreign currency.

However, the role of tradition differed between Pemba and the mainland. Educational officers and teachers in Pemba argued that traditional pubertal teachings among some ethnic groups, and the traditional belief that girls should marry at puberty, contribute to the pregnancy problem. Some teachers on the mainland argued in the opposite direction. The breakdown of traditional societies in Tanzania, intermarriage and migration from rural to urban areas have all contributed to the problem, since adolescent girls lack good models.

The issues at stake

School-girl pregnancy has negative consequences not only for the girls and their children, but also for the society at large. The girls lose their chances of finishing their education and thereby the possibility of gaining good and well-paid employment. The parents lose all the money they have invested in their daughters' education and future. The resources that the state has devoted to the training of the young girls is wasted when the girls are expelled from school and are unable to pursue their education.

One significant problem in connection with schoolgirl pregnancy is puberty rites. After going through the ceremony, the girls are considered by society to have attained the status of reproductive adults and are expected to behave as such. Hence, suggestions have been made that the puberty rites should not be held until the girls have finished school. State punishment of those who prevent girls from completing their education and the compulsory nature of universal primary education suggest the regulation of reproductive activities by the state. The state assumes control of the girls' sexual powers until they have finished school. Traditionally, mothers had the responsibility of guarding their girls and making sure that they did not fall pregnant before they were married. Now that girls can go to school and take part in many social activities outside the home, it is almost impossible for the mothers or anybody else to keep a close eye on them.

It is in the interests of the parents that their daughters do not fall pregnant while at school. Apart from the fact that the pregnancy may ruin the girl's educational future, it may not be easy for her to find a husband if the father of the child refuses to marry her. This would mean the loss of bridewealth to the parents. The girls, for their part, are tempted by the money and other luxuries provided by the men who are invariably older than them. They see these relationships as a means of improving their lot and of escaping the poverty that engulfs them.

Unfortunately, these girls do not seem to get much support from other older males in their society, including their own fathers. The fathers, religious leaders and community elders turn their backs on the needs of the younger generation. They do not take any steps to protect the youth from the dangers of adolescent life. Instead, they are prepared to risk the sexual and reproductive health of the youth to uphold their own principles.

References

Freyhold, M.V., 1977, *UPE and Education for Self Reliance*. TIRDEP Evaluation Report on School Buildings Programme.

Kalunga, E.T., 1988, *The Factors Associated with Girls' Attitudes towards Science in Tanzania*. Unpublished M.A. dissertation, University of Bristol.

Katunzi, N.B. and Sumra, S., 1992, *The effect of the re-introduction of school fees on girls' education*. WED Report No. 5. Dar es Salaam.

Mbilinyi M., Mbughuni F., Meena R., Olekambaine P., 1991, *Education in Tanzania with a gender perspective*. Education Division Documents No. 53. Stockholm: SIDA.

Mwanze, R.M., 1991, *Women and Higher Education in Zanzibar*. Unpublished M.A. dissertation, University of Birmingham.

Ndabi,D.M., 1987, *The Perspective Validity of Secondary Education Examination*. Dar es Salaam: National Examination Council of Tanzania.

Sekwao, C., 1989, Women in Technical Education: A Survey of Factors Influencing the Participation of Women in Technical Education, Training and Jobs (Tanzania). Report sponsored by Commonwealth Association of Polytechnics in Africa.

Sumra, S., 1985, *Primary Education and Transition to Socialism in Rural Tanzania*. Unpublished Ph.D. dissertation, Stanford University.

Turley, O.W. and Twatson, M., 1978, *A History of Education in East Africa*. New York: NOK.

United Republic of Tanzania, 1992, *Women and Men in Tanzania*. Dar es Salaam: Bureau of Statistics.

Wizara ya Elimu, 1991, *Hotuba ya Waziri wa Elimu Mheshimiwa Omari Mapuri Kuhusu Makadirio ya Fedha kwa Mwaka 1991–92*. Zanzibar: Serikali ya Mapinduzi.

4. Arranged marriages

Rosalia S. Katapa

Arranged marriages exist in many Third World countries. The reasons for them vary within and among countries. In such marriages, negotiations usually take place between the parents of a teenage girl and the prospective husband. If he is also a teenager, arrangements are made between his parents and the girl's parents. In all the countries where arranged marriages are practised, the bride-to-be is almost always a teenager.

People in many parts of mainland Tanzania, and almost all of Zanzibar, practise arranged marriages. Among the Wakurya in mainland Tanzania, bridewealth is paid in cows to the bride's parents. The number of cows to be paid depends on the outcome of the negotiations between the families. Marriage takes place only after bridewealth, or a part of it, has been paid. If all the bridewealth cannot be paid before marriage, it is paid later in instalments.

Several weeks before the wedding, the whole community is informed of the coming event. The day before the wedding, a ceremony takes place at the home of the bride's parents. All the people in the bride's village, as well as the groom, his friends and relatives, attend the ceremony. The activities include dancing, feasting and drinking the local brew. On the wedding day, the ceremony shifts to the groom's home. When the ceremony is over (usually the day after the wedding), the bride's friends and relatives go back to their village, leaving the bride behind.

Female and male circumcision is part of the Wakurya culture. It is performed when the girls and boys are about twelve to fourteen years old. Girls and boys can get married after they have passed through a circumcision ceremony.

While in Zanzibar, I was informed that marriages there were contracted according to the Islamic religion and that it was the responsibility of the father (or a paternal grandfather) to find a husband for his daughter. I was also told that marrying a blood relative was acceptable, provided the fathers of the young couple are not brothers, or their mothers are not sisters. The reason for this restriction is that if a father dies, his brother becomes a guardian of his children. Similarly, if a mother dies, her sister becomes a guardian of her children. One cannot be a guardian and a father- or mother-in-law at the same time.

There is an extreme variation in levels of child-bearing among teenagers within and among regions. The maternal mortality rate is higher for teenagers than for women between twenty and thirty-five years. Recent demographic and health surveys conducted in more than ten African countries have shown that the infant mortality rate is higher among infants born to teenage mothers than among those born to older women.

Arranged marriages and teenage reproduction

Many teenage girls comply when they learn of the arrangement of their marriages. However, there are some who resist in different ways, such as refusing and/or running away (Rwezaura, 1982); others elope with their boy-friends, and in extreme cases there are those who commit suicide.

Reports are to be found in Tanzania's daily newspapers about deaths which occur as a result of teenage love, marriages and abortions. The following are a few examples of reports of such deaths which appeared while this research was being conducted.

In Musoma, an eighty-six year old man committed suicide by hanging himself when he suspected that his sixteen year old wife was involving herself in extra marital sex with a young man residing in the same house as the couple. (Mfanyakazi, 4 May 1991:16)

A Form Two girl at a day secondary school run by the Roman Catholic church in Arusha committed suicide to protest against a forced marriage. She was reported to have swallowed thirty quinine tablets. (Daily News, 29 October 1991)

In Mbeya, a nineteen year old girl died after taking an overdose of chloroquine tablets. It was reported that she swallowed the tablets

*after her brother demanded an explanation about the places she had
been spending the previous nights. (Daily News, 30 October 1991)*

Commenting about another teenage death, the *Daily News* had
this to say: "This is the fourth time in a week for young women to
commit suicide" (*Daily News*, 31 October 1991). All the four
teenage deaths were marriage or love related.

*In Tanga, a twenty-one year old woman died after taking an
excessive dose of chloroquine tablets, allegedly in an abortion
attempt; she was already a mother of two. (Uhuru, 2 November
1991; Daily News, 2 November 1991)*

On the other hand, some teenagers in arranged marriages are
comfortable and happy. It is not possible to cite newspaper quotations
on "happy and successful arranged marriages" because these cases
are hardly ever reported to journalists.

Approaching teenagers and their parents

It has been pointed out that pregnant teenagers face many health-
related problems as compared to older women, and that the rate of
survival of their babies is lower than that of babies of older women.
Realizing these facts, one wonders why teenage girls become pregnant. There are probably many explanations for the problem of
teenage pregnancy in Tanzania. One of them is arranged marriages.

Upon marriage, most teenage wives are not allowed to use
contraceptives. The reason is that they are expected to become
pregnant and prove their fertility to society.

My main objective was to study arranged marriages. I did the
following:
– I explored the attitudes of teenage girls and their parents towards
  arranged marriages
– I assessed the amount of knowledge that teenage girls and their
  parents have on reproductive health problems which occur because
  of early marriages
– I observed the handling of marital cases involving teenage wives by
  the social welfare department and the law courts. The marital cases

involved teenage wives both as complainants, and as the accused.

I decided to go to the Wakurya in Tarime district in the lake-zone of Tanzania as well as to Jambiani, Zanzibar, because I felt that in mainland Tanzania arranged marriages were more prevalent among the Wakurya than among other tribes.

Unlike most of mainland Tanzania, which is chiefly inhabited by black Africans, the main inhabitants of Zanzibar are black Africans, Indians and Arabs. This is primarily the result of the Arab slave trade in East Africa and the Arab colonization of Zanzibar. I selected Jambiani ward in the southern district of Zanzibar as an area occupied by black Africans only.

I observed people's behaviour and their surroundings. I also participated in informal discussions with village leaders, elders and women as well as with school teachers, court and social welfare officers.

I used three questionnaires designed respectively for teenage girls, parents of teenage girls and teenage wives. In each of the two regions, I met forty school- and non-school-going teenage girls, thirty parents (fifteen mothers and fifteen fathers) and ten teenage wives. I wish to emphasize that I myself filled in every questionnaire and that the schoolgirl, the parent or teenage wife was the only other person present at the interview.

I found those eighty people by using a government structure. The smallest unit in the government's administrative structure is a ten-cell. Each ten-cell usually consists of ten households and it is headed by a ten-cell leader. About fifty to one hundred ten-cells make up a village and three or four villages make up a ward. In each ward, the ward secretary has a list of all ten-cell leaders. Thus, with the assistance of the ward secretary, I visited many ten-cell leaders and in the process identified the people to be interviewed. I went to see three schools in the areas and selected some school teenage girls to answer a questionnaire.

At the social welfare and primary court offices, my assistant and I went through a pile of case files. My aim was to identify cases which concerned teenage girls or wives. I did the collection of case records after the administration of the questionnaires. All data were collected in 1991.

Arranged marriages in the Wakurya society

Wakurya teenage girls

The forty teenage girls were born, brought up and lived in Tarime district. Their ages ranged from thirteen to nineteen years. More than 80 per cent of them were Christians. At the time these research data were collected, 20 per cent of them had lost their fathers and none of them had lost a mother. All but two of the rest had parents who were still married and they were living with them.

Out of the forty teenage girls, only four were aware of the existence of Tanzania's *Law of Marriage Act* of 1971 (LMA). In that act, marriage is defined as "the voluntary union of man and woman intending to last for their joint lives". Section 25 (d) of this law states that "where the parties belong to a community or to communities which follow customary laws, the marriage can be contracted in civil form or according to the rites of the customary law". In many customary laws, marriage can be defined as "the union of a man and a woman", i.e., it can be voluntary or involuntary.

The LMA specifies that the minimum age of marriage for a girl is eighteen years. At fifteen, a girl can get married with her parents' consent and for a fourteen year old girl to get married, special permission is required. On the other hand, customary laws do not have a minimum age at which girls can get married.

Four of the girls interviewed correctly mentioned eighteen and fifteen years as being the ages at which a girl could respectively marry without and with her parents' consent. Three of them had learned this from their church's confirmation classes, and the other one had read this in a book she had bought at her church.

All the teenage girls were aware of the existence of arranged marriages in their tribe. Two-thirds of them attributed this practice to the desire of fathers to get bridewealth (cows).

Less than half of the teenage girls indicated that they would like to get married when they grew older. Almost all of those who aspired to get married also wanted bridewealth to be paid for them, and half of them preferred arranged marriages. Moreover, three of them favoured polygamous marriages because they felt that co-wives would assist them with household chores and childcare.

Two teenage girls felt that it was too early to start thinking about getting married in the future. This is quite noteworthy because they were seventeen and nineteen years old. Moreover, the nineteen year old had finished her primary school education. The remaining teenage girls never wanted to get married. Actually, I observed that they "feared marriage". Each one of them was uncomfortable when discussing the marriage issue. The reasons they gave for not aspiring to marriage are presented below.

Table 14. *Wakurya girls who do not want to marry*

Reason	No. of girls
Wants to be a nun	7
Fear of leading difficult lives	4
Fear of hard work and being beaten	3
Fear of being mistreated	1
Wants to avoid quarrels	1
Fear of childbirth	1
Interested in further education	1
Just not interested	1
Total	19

After a long discussion with each of the teenage girls who did not want to get married, I came to the conclusion that they all feared it. They associated marriage with hard labour and cruelty at the hands of their husbands. Those who claimed they wanted to be nuns felt that this was the only escape from marriage. Even some of the girls who had marital aspirations acknowledged that most marriages are associated with hard labour and beatings by husbands. They also felt that marriage was an inescapable duty.

Rearing cattle, milking cows, cleaning stables, growing food crops and harvesting coffee are among the tasks of a Wakurya wife. Certainly, moving cattle to and fro in search of grazing is not an easy task, and neither is hand-hoe farming. It is no wonder the Wakurya teenage girls associated marriage with hard labour.

Teenage girls were more aware of the socio-economic problems than the reproductive health problems that affect teenage wives. About half of them were able to say something on socio-economic problems. Such problems identified by them were: failure to manage household work; not having enough food; beatings by the husband; poor communication with the husband; and inability to care for babies. On the other hand, only 20 per cent of the teenage girls said anything about the reproductive health problems affecting teenage wives. The problems they identified were: not being able to have a child for a long time; child delivery; the possibility of dying during childbirth; and/or delivering an unhealthy or premature baby. Not a single girl aged thirteen or fourteen years had anything to say about reproductive health issues.

I asked each teenage girl about the advice she would give to a friend who was not interested in the marriage her parents were arranging for her. More than half of them would advise the friend to refuse the marriage. Half of the remaining ones would advise her to request the elders to talk the issue over with the parents; the other half would advise her to accept her parents' decision.

Wakurya parents

Almost all the parents in the sample had married daughters, as well as teenage and younger daughters. Most of them (70 per cent) were Christians. The number of children the mothers had ever given birth to ranged from four to twelve. As for the fathers, the number of their children ranged from eight to thirty-nine. This is not surprising because polygamy is quite common in Wakurya society.

All the parents were aware of the existence of arranged marriages in their tribe and some of them had participated in arranging marriages for their daughters. Many of them (60 per cent) felt that obtaining bridewealth (cows) was the main reason for arranging marriages for teenage daughters. Most of them (90 per cent) felt that if a daughter refused an arranged marriage, they would let her make her own choice. However, if the marriage failed, the daughter would only have herself to blame. Some parents were allowing their daughters to find their own fiancés.

About half of the parents seemed to be aware of the existence of the *Law of Marriage Act* of 1971. However, only one of them was fully conversant with the contents of the act–she had secondary school education. She was the ward court chairperson (an unpaid community activity).

Incompetence in household work and in communication with husbands ranked high among parents' responses to the question of the socio-economic problems that befall teenage wives. The other problems mentioned were the difficulty of life because of economic hardship, fear of husbands and mental immaturity. Only six parents said something about reproductive health. The problems mentioned were bad health because of pregnancy, child delivery and the possiblity of having a miscarriage or an unhealthy baby.

When I asked the parents whether they had heard of teenagers who had had miscarriages, premature or underweight babies, or stillborns, they agreed that they had heard of these things and some of them had actually witnessed such phenomena. Many of them had also heard of teenagers who had died during delivery.

Marital history of the mothers

All the mothers, except one, had married while they were under twenty. Some of them could not remember the age at which they had married but they were sure they had been under fifteen. One had married at twenty, and she was the only one with secondary school education.

Four out of fifteen female parents claimed that they had had a say in their marriages. The other eleven, including the one with secondary school education, had had their marriages arranged for them by their parents.

At the time of their first marriages, eleven of them married single men, three married men who had other wives, and one married a divorcee. At the time of this research, nine of the female parents were still married and the other six were widows.

Most of the mothers had had their first babies within two years of marriage. One of them recounted her experience in these terms: "I married at the age of thirteen. I then had seven consecutive miscarriages. I now have eleven children."

Wakurya teenage wives

The ten teenage wives who were selected for this research were born, brought up and lived in Tarime. They were all still married to their first husbands and all of them had married Wakurya men. Seven of them had married young single men while two had married middle-aged men. The marriage of one of the middle-aged men to his teenage wife was his second one. The other middle-aged man was a Moslem and he had already informed his teenage wife that their marriage could become polygamous later on.

Eight of the ten teenage wives claimed that they had chosen their own husbands. However, one of them warned me that, "in many cases nowadays, by the time a man approached you for marriage, he has already talked to your parents. He will not tell you that he has already talked to them". One teenager admitted that hers was an arranged marriage.

The bridewealth paid for nine teenage wives ranged from fifteen to twenty-five cows. One husband had paid nine cows and was left with a debt of six cows to pay to his in-laws. Thirty-five thousand shillings (equivalent to several cows) were given as bridewealth for the tenth teenage wife.

None of the teenage wives was aware of the existence of the Law of *Marriage Act*, neither at the time of their marriages, nor at the time I saw them.

After marriage, only one out of the ten teenage wives tried to postpone pregnancy by using contraceptives. She conceived soon after having stopped using the pill. At the time I saw them, seven out of the ten teenage wives were already mothers and another one had experienced a miscarriage. Their age at marriage ranged from fifteen to eighteen years, and those who were mothers had given birth to their first born between the ages of sixteen and nineteen. The teenage mothers claimed that they had not faced problems during delivery and that their babies had been born healthy, although one of them had delivered by caesarian section.

Primary court and social welfare cases

At Nyamwaga primary court there were more marriage-related cases than criminal ones. In the gold mining village of Nyamongo, most of the complainants in marriage-related cases were women. Once a man struck a fortune in the mine, he might even marry five wives. However, divorce would be just around the corner. The duration of such marriages was usually two years. Hence, men in the mining area were not generally serious about marriage. Women went to court to complain about mistreatment and/or to demand explanations as to why their husbands were divorcing them. In this mining village, there was also a significant number of marriages involving schoolgirls.

In the agricultural area (the northern part of Nyamwaga ward), men were usually the complainants in marriage-related cases. In this area, many old fathers married off their daughters to their fellow old men. However, after some time, some of the young wives eloped with young men. Thus the old men (husbands) went to court to demand their bridewealth back.

The refund of bridewealth depended on who was at fault. In many cases in Nyamongo, the decision was that there should be no refund of bridewealth. This was because it had been proved that the husbands had contributed significantly to the marriage breakdown. In cases of eloping young wives, bridewealth was being refunded. However, if she had children by the ex-husband, in most cases the refund was reduced, e.g., half of the cows were returned.

People went to the social welfare department for reconciliation. If the conciliation board failed to reconcile a couple, it sent their case to a law court. A case from the primary court and three cases from the social welfare files are presented below.

Case No 1. A 1991 primary court case:

Lizee was seventy-eight years old, and he filed a divorce case against his seventeen year old wife called Kadogo. The couple had married in 1989 after thirty-six cows had been paid as bridewealth.

During the marriage they managed to have one child, a son. After some time, the wife found a boy-friend, flirted with him for some time, and then eloped with him.

In January 1991, the husband went to the primary court for a divorce. It was granted. He then requested a refund of his bridewealth but the court's decision was that no part of the bridewealth would be returned to him. The reason given was that when he decided to marry at the age of seventy-six years, he knew very well that it would be difficult to live with such a young girl. Hence, he had contributed to the separation, and eventually the divorce. The husband appealed to the district court, which later upheld the primary court's decision. He finally appealed to the high court, which also upheld the primary court's decision.

I consider the decision in this case as a landmark on the teenage girl–old men's marriage issue.

Case No 2. A 1991 social welfare case:

Msiwati was an eighteen year old wife who filed a complaint against her sixty-two year old husband, Mjukuu. They had married in 1989 after bridewealth of fourteen cows had been paid.

The wife claimed that she was being returned to her parents by the husband. She wanted to know why. In his defence, the husband claimed that she frequently ran away. He thus had decided to send her back to her parents and to claim a refund of his bridewealth of fourteen cows. At the time I was there, the conciliation board was still waiting for witnesses.

Case No 3. A 1991 social welfare case:

Seventeen year old Kasichana filed a complaint against her seventeen year old husband called Kavulana. The couple married in 1989. The bridewealth paid was twelve cows.

The wife had been chased away from their matrimonial home with all her belongings. She was interested in going back to her husband. According to him, the wife used to run away frequently. He felt that even if he went back home with her, she would still run away.

The conciliation board noted that the marriage was arranged by the parents. Instead of both sets of parents assisting the young couple, they had contributed to the problems that made the marriage unstable. Because of the parents' interference, it appeared that the marriage would not last. Hence, the case was sent to the ward for onward transmission to the primary court.

Case No 4. A 1990 social welfare case:

Fifteen year old Mtoto filed a complaint against her husband Wakosawa, aged sixteen years. The couple had married in 1988. The husband had paid nine cows as bridewealth, and he still had to pay nine more cows.

The wife wanted to dissolve the marriage because of frequent beatings and abuse. He still wanted his wife and was against dissolving their marriage.

It was remarked in the file that the husband did not appear at the last conciliation session. Thus, the case was still in progress.

The cases presented above show that some arranged marriages are problematic. The problems include being chased away and in other cases being demanded back. It is clear that an arranged marriage takes place between a teenage girl and a man of any age.

Between January and May 1991, there were also ten *mkamwana* marriage cases in the primary court. These marriages are not recognized by the *Law of Marriage Act* of 1971, but they exist in the Wakurya society (Rwezaura, 1982).

An *mkamwana* marriage can be defined as a relationship between an elderly woman without a son and a girl. The elderly woman pays bridewealth to the parents of a girl, then a "marriage" takes place. The girl is then said to be an mkamwana of the sonless woman. *Mkamwana* is a Kiswahili word which means daughter-in-law. However, in the Wakurya society, an mkamwana marriage means a relationship as explained above.

After an *mkamwana* marriage has taken place, the sonless elderly woman allocates a man (usually a married man in her clan) to the "bride" and children born of this relationship will belong to her. The children are referred to as the "grandchildren" of the sonless elderly woman. It is believed that *mkamwana* marriages bring social security to sonless elderly women in the patriarchal Wakurya society. The prevalence of *mkamwana* marriages is very low. It is assumed that they are being phased out.

Arranged marriages in Jambiani, Zanzibar

Jambiani is a rural coastal area in the southern district in Zanzibar. All the residents of Jambiani are Moslems. The *Law of Marriage Act* of 1971 does not apply to Zanzibar. Instead, the Islamic law applies to all Moslem Zanzibaris. This being the case, I did not ask questions regarding the *Law of Marriage Act*.

Jambiani teenage girls

The forty teenage girls who were selected for this research were residents of Jambiani. All of them, except eight, had been born and brought up in Jambiani. The other eight had been born elsewhere on Zanzibar. Parents of twenty-two of them were still married, but only ten of the couples were living with their daughters. Three teenage girls had lost their fathers and another one had lost her mother. The mother of one of the teenage girls had never been married.

Almost all the girls were aware of the existence of arranged marriages in Zanzibar. All of them aspired to be married and some of them were already engaged. Three out of four girls indicated that they would prefer to go into arranged marriages. One girl stated, that since she had lost her father, she would be obliged to find a husband on her own. The other girls maintained that they would prefer to look for husbands on their own. The girls who preferred arranged marriages stated that parents cared for their daughters. Most of the girls preferred monogamous marriages, several others preferred polygamous marriages, and the remaining ones felt that either type of marriage would be acceptable to them. Those who preferred polygamous marriages stated that they would have the company of co-wives who would assist them with household chores and childcare.

Almost half the teenage girls said something on the reproductive health problems which befell teenage wives. The problems they identified were difficulties of child delivery, caesarian section, delivery of an unhealthy or premature baby, and the possibility of death of the mother or the new born or both. Only a few of them said something about socio-economic problems. Those mentioned had to do with failure to manage household work, not being supplied with enough food and not being able to take care of the babies.

Jambiani parents

All thirty parents that I talked to were aware of the existence of arranged marriages in Zanzibar. Nearly all of them said that the best way to ensure that a daughter got a good husband was to arrange a marriage for her. Only a few said that they would not mind if their daughters decided to look for their own husbands. However, in case of problems cropping up in the marriages, the daughters would have themselves to blame. It was claimed that arranged marriages last because the parents have scrutinized the man before accepting him as their daughter's husband. Most parents felt that the main motive for arranging marriages while the girls were still young was to prevent premarital sex. Half of the parents would not mind whether their daughters went into monogamous or polygamous marriages. Several mothers insisted that polygamy was an imposition on first wives, and it was not to their liking.

The replies given by parents to the question as to what they would do if their daughters refused an arranged marriage are presented below.

Table 15. *What Jambiani parents would do if a daughter refused an arranged marriage*

Response	No. of parents	Percent
Force her to marry the man	10	33.3
Respect her decision	8	26.7
Convince her to marry the man	3	10.0
Wait until they find a likeable man	2	6.6
It has never happened so why speculate?	1	3.3
It has never happened and never will	1	3.3
Total	25	83.2

It is encouraging to see that some of them would respect their daughters' decisions.

Some parents were aware of the following health problems which affected teenage wives: injury during sexual intercourse, pregnancy being a cause of bad health, difficulties at childbirth and miscarriages. However, some of them stated that these problems befell older women too.

A few parents mentioned socio-economic problems which teenage wives face. The problems were incompetence in household work and being mistreated by husbands.

Most parents felt that the main reason for arranging marriages while girls were still young was to prevent premarital sex. The girls who preferred arranged marriages stated that the parents cared for them. Maelezo, Dar es Salaam

Marital history of the mothers

All the first marriages of the mothers had been arranged for them. Four out of the fifteen female parents had married while they were under thirteen years of age, another one married at the age of twenty and the remaining ones married while they were teenagers. Three out of the four female parents who had married while they were under thirteen had had their first babies while they were still thirteen. Two others had had their first born when they were fourteen, while most of them had become mothers for the first time within two years of marriage. The numbers of children they had ever given birth to ranged from one to ten.

Four mothers had experienced the following reproductive problems:
– I married at the age of twelve and had a miscarriage at the age of thirteen years
– I married at the age of ten, that was before puberty. I had a still birth at the age of thirteen years
– I married at the age of fifteen. The following year I delivered a child who survived for a few hours only
– I married when I was very young. I stayed for many years without having a child. I now have six children.

At that time, nine female parents were still in their first marriages, three others were in their second or third, and the remaining three were divorcees.

Jambiani teenage wives

The ten teenage wives were residing in Jambiani. Six of them had been born and brought up there, and the other four had been born somewhere else on Zanzibar.

Five teenage wives were in arranged marriages. Four others claimed to have chosen their own husbands. However, three of them were pregnant when they married and the fourth married after the child was born. The tenth one did not provide any information on her marital history. All the teenage wives except one had married single men. The one exception had married a middle-aged man who already had a wife. The bridewealth paid for them ranged from one thousand to eight thousand shillings (at the time of this research, three hundred shillings was equivalent to one U.S. dollar).

When I visited them, seven out of the ten wives were already mothers. The age of marriage ranged from fourteen to nineteen years, and the age at the birth of their first borns ranged from fifteen to nineteen years. All the young mothers claimed that they had not faced any problems during childbirth and that their babies had been born healthy. Four of them had given birth in health institutions, and the other three had had home deliveries.

None of the seven mothers had used contraceptives before having their first babies, and the other three wives were not using contraceptives.

Almost all the teenage wives were engaged in planting and harvesting a seaweed called *mwani*. The income from this activity was quite good. Some of them were also making hats as their second economic activity. Nine of them said arranged marriages were good, and one girl could not make up her mind about whether they were good or bad.

My views on arranged marriages

Parents from both research areas were more aware than their teenage daughters of reproductive health and socio-economic problems which affect teenage wives. It may be because the parents had experienced some of these difficulties themselves during the early years of their own marriages. Teenage girls under fifteen years were not able to identify any reproductive health problems. This could be due to their tender age.

Wakurya: None of the ten teenage wives whom I met were married to very old men, nor were they in *mkamwana* marriages. It is believed that very old men and sonless elderly women who marry girls are very protective of their teenage wives. This could be the reason why I could not visit teenage wives in these marital arrangements.

According to Rwezaura (1982) one of the main reasons for arranging marriages is because the bridewealth the girl's family receives is in turn used to "fetch" a wife for her brother. However, economic hardships are playing a significant role in reducing the prevalence of arranged marriages. Discussions with the elders indicated that, in the past, bridewealth could exceed fifty cows. In this research, bridewealth paid for teenage wives ranged from fifteen to twenty-five cows. With increasing divorces of teenage wives, some fathers are being asked to refund the bridewealth. Some husbands go to law courts, only to find themselves forfeiting their claim on the bridewealth. Thus, arranged marriages are not as attractive to fathers and husbands as they used to be in the past.

It is obvious from the above cases that some teenagers marry very old men. One possible impact of these marriages is that children lose their fathers while they are still young. I found that 20 per cent of the Wakurya teenage girls that I interviewed had lost their fathers, and none of them had lost a mother.

Jambiani: Bride-price is very low, the reason behind arranged marriages being to fulfil religious obligations. However, there were parents who felt that in the rare event that a daughter refused an arranged marriage, they would be prepared to discuss the issue and resolve it.

It appears that the divorce rate in Jambiani is high. One-third of the teenage girls' parents were divorced. It also appears that it is common practice for children to live with relatives even if both parents are still alive and still married. Six out of fifteen mothers were either divorcees or on their second marriages. This suggests the existence of a relationship between low bridewealth and high divorce rate.

In Jambiani, too, parents were more aware of reproductive health problems than their teenage daughters and the teenage wives. Moreover, the parents' fear that the girls might engage in premarital sex if they were not married early enough was not baseless. Out of the ten teenage wives, one married after having a child and three others were pregnant at marriage.

Conclusion

To my understanding, in Jambiani parents arrange marriages for their daughters to fulfil religious obligations. This being the case, arranged marriages will persist in Jambiani. However, one needs to find out the age at which it is reasonable for married girls to start indulging in sexual activities.

On the other hand, I feel that arranged marriages in the Wakurya society are a result of tribal culture. My study has indicated that the prevalence of arranged marriages in the Wakurya society is low as compared with the past. In my opinion, the prevalence of arranged marriages in Wakurya society will decrease if certain socio-economic conditions prevail. Some of these conditions are economic hardship, improvements in divorce law (e.g., non-refund of bridewealth when a teenage girl–old man marriage breaks up) and division of family assets when marriage breaks up. In addition, improvements should be made to the Wakurya customary laws by deleting those that oppress women. Lastly, the *mkamwana* marriages should be eliminated.

References

Bureau of Statistics, 1973, *Demographic Survey of Tanzania.*

Bureau of Statistics, 1978, *Population Census of Tanzania, Vol. V, Fertility and Mortality Data for Rural and Urban Areas of Regions.* Dar es Salaam: Planning Commission.

Bureau of Statistics, 1978, *Population Census of Tanzania, Vol. VII, Basic Demographic and Socio-economic characteristics.* Dar es Salaam: Planning Commission.

Demographic and health surveys of Botswana, Burundi, Ghana, Liberia, Mali, Nigeria (Ondo state), Zimbabwe, Uganda. Published by each country's Ministry of Health Bureau of Statistics.

Kandiah, Vasantha, 1989, *Data on Child Bearing by Women under 20 World Wide.* Notes from the seminar series, The Determinants and Consequences of Female Headed Households. London: The Population Council.

Katapa, R.S., 1992, *Arranged marriages and teenage reproductive health.* Research report. University of Dar es Salaam.

Mbilinyi, M.J., 1969, *The Study of Attitudes of Tanzanian Girls and their Fathers towards Education.* Institute of Education, University of Dar es Salaam.

Rwezaura, B.A., 1982, *Social and legal change in Kuria family relations.* Unpublished Ph.D. thesis, University of Warwick.

Rwezaura, B.A., 1985, *Traditional Family Law and Change in Tanzania: A Study of the Kuria Social System.* Baden-Baden: Nomas Verlags Gesellschaft.

Tanzania, 1971, *Law of Marriage Act.*

5. The initiation rite

Mary Ntukula

The initiation rite is an institution concerned with the regeneration and continuity of life and thus also with the particular contributions of women and men. The rites enact a symbolic rebirth when the initiates attain the new status of adulthood. Such important rites of passage over the course of the individual's lifespan are widespread in African societies. Their form and content vary. Different ethnic groups have their own ways of preparing their children for womanhood and manhood. The advent of puberty marks the transition to adulthood. The initiation ceremony was one of the devices by which the community passed on knowledge and symbolic metaphors to the young about the meaning and practical implications of marriage and the continuity of the clan. Initiation rites used to be important moulders of personality.

In the early days, the recipients of these instructions were expected to marry immediately after initiation. In the societies I studied, the approved mode of mating is through marriage, and the family is responsible for ensuring that their children get married before indulging in sexual relationships. This is achieved by offering special instructions during initiation ceremonies.

Although symbols of and metaphors for fertility permeate African cosmologies of life there is no word for fertility in most African languages, nor any abstract concept of fertility or creativity (Jacobson-Widding and van Beek, 1990). Instead the cultural anthropologists have identified

a rich symbolic language expressing the characteristics and location of those forces or power that men are supposed to exploit whenever they want to create something new—be it in human lives, new crops, new strength, or new products. (Jacobson-Widding and van Beek, 1990:15)

Where are the sources of fertility then found?

All over sub-Saharan Africa, the sky is connected with male powers of creativity, while the earth is perceived as a female source of fertility. Thus, when the powers "high up" are ritually fused with those "low down", the resultant creative process is also perceived as an amalgamation of male and female. The merging of the two elements will erase the hierarchial distinction between man and woman, and between all social categories that are classified as "high" versus "low", "superior" versus "inferior". To transcend duality and hierarchy by merging opposed categories, seems to be at the heart of African notions of fertility. (Jacobson-Widding and van Beek, 1990:21)

At the level of implicit notions, people give much attention to female spirits who live deep down in the water of the earth. In daily life, it is common to find that containers made of the clay from the low and moist parts of the earth are treated as symbols of female creativity.

It is intriguing to find throughout the region the prevalence of androgynous ideas about how a human being is constituted, i.e., how persons are perceived as having both female and male characteristics. Thus, androgynous deities are connected with creation and fertility.

Generally, "their creative powers are conceived of as primordial units, which represent the fusion of heaven and earth, male and female, and whose unity must be recreated each time that life is to be regenerated". (Jacobsson-Widding and van Beek, 1990:22)

In any process of creation the opposite elements of womanhood and malehood are fused in a ritual enacting of physical love between woman and man. This symbolic act of creation is carried out whenever something new is to be shaped – a new tool, a new agricultural season, a new child, a new pot, a new meal. (Jacobson-Widding and van Beek, 1990:22)

The idea of creation seemed to have penetrated African worldviews. Nowadays, the whole approach is different. Conception is no longer expressed as a renewal of the community, or the rebirth of ancestors. The unity between human beings, animals and plants

In the past, the aim of initiation rites was to integrate the youth into the moral order. Today, modernization has taken instruction on sexuality out of the social and cultural context.
Private photo.

is broken. The current language emhasizes values such as sexual and reproductive health, which are confined within the framework of modern medicine. However, the centrality of sexuality remains, although it has been deprived of much of its former meaning.

The initiation ceremony is in itself recognized as an instructional and tuitional device. It is a socially accepted means of passing on knowledge and values concerning procreation, mores, sexual skills, spacing and prevention of unwanted pregnancies – or what is today called "fertility regulation". As soon as a girl is able to conceive, she has to be prepared for all that is implied in womanhood.

Collective and individual rites of transition

One can distinguish between collective and individual forms of initiation. The collective or public initiation rites are organized when several girls have attained puberty and the ceremony can be performed for all of them. The initiation of boys takes place simultaneously, but separately, at another place. As the reproductive roles of women and men differ, so do the instructions given to each gender. *Unyago* is the term used for female initiation (Cory, 1956). In the field, I learned that male initiation is called *jando.*

It is still common at collective initiations for the initiates and their instructors to go into the bush or forest, and to stay there for a period ranging from three days to several weeks. This period is followed by seclusion *(kumweka mwali ndani).* It is rare for *individual* initiates to go to the bush.

Individual initiation is conducted within the family. The leaders of this private ceremony are usually close relatives of the initiate: aunts, grandparents, sisters and cousins. However, parents are excluded from performing this role. The families may hire a recognized initiation leader to conduct the ceremony in the family.

The group of girls (and boys) who were initiated together by a member of their clan and descent group form their own support network throughout their adult lives. They have mutual obligations towards each other. Individual initiation does not create such bonds of future support.

According to cultural anthropologists (Jacobson-Widding et al., 1990) there is an "official model" of social relationships in most African cultures which recognizes the social communion of those who trace common descent, actual or fictive, from the ancestors of a named clan.

The idea implicit in this model is "that we are all one" and share a common "self". At the heart of this notion of a collective self we may trace an ideal of absence of boundaries between particular individual . selves – or between particular social categories constituting a lineage. (Jacobson-Widding and van Beek, 1990:34)

The authors remind us, that they are describing an ideal model of connectedness and belonging, rather than real interaction in everyday life.

Jacobson-Widding *et al.* look for explanations for the creation of collective versus individualistic selves. They argue that the sense of social connectedness within a culturally defined collectivity that transcends the boundaries of the immediate family and lineage seems to be intimately linked with a religious concern for the land. As soon as the basis for social communion disappears, subsistence apparently becomes a matter of individual enterprise and rationality, rather than a symbolic enterprise for the continuity and survival of the community as a whole.

Hence, these antropologists conclude that the presence or absence of a collectivistic social ideology seems to be intrinsically connected with ritual versus rational attitudes towards the management of renewable sources of subsistence and wealth. Accordingly, the distinction between collective and individual fertility rites –including subsistence as well as pubertal initiation – is related to conditions such as collective or individual rights to land, and to the stability or flux of populations, collapses within established markets, and the disintegration of larger communities, in other words, the same circumstances that have contributed to the disappearance of initiation.

Talking to *"somos"* and initiates

I wanted to know more about traditional institutions for fertility control in relation to adolescent pregnancies by looking into the survival of initiation rites. My interest focused on fertility regulation in the past as well as at present. In a sense, this is a rather limited approach to the question of how young girls did and do deal with their fertility and protect themselves against pregnancy during casual sexual relationships. I conclude by commenting on the absence of proper institutions that can assume responsibility for reproduction under contemporary conditions.

I try to highlight my findings by including excerpts from anthropological literature on African folk-models of fertility and personhood, so as to reveal a neglected past that might be instructive about present conditions.

To achieve my aims, I have used four local "initiation leaders" and one traditional practitioner as my informants. I have also been able to select single initiated girls for interview in order to obtain more details. Other girls that I interviewed were pupils of a secondary school in Songea. Altogether I talked to forty-eight girls between thirteen and nineteen years. These comprise the main participants, since initiation involves instructors on one side and novices or initiates on the other. I also had the opportunity to observe two initiation ceremonies and one send-off ceremony.

"*Somo*" is a Kiswahili word. It means initiation instructor or mistress of initiation, the ceremonial leader, the expert on initiation rites. The somo has a recognized status within the community as being knowledgeable and the master in the field of initiation. She should never be an immediate relative of the initiates. *Mkasano, mnandi, mhunga* and *mkole* are Luguru words for various initiation leaders who have different roles.

The *somo* and the *mhunga* have the crucial role of organizing and leading the rite. They usually have a charismatic personality and act like leaders. Each action is performed according to their directives. The novice, i.e., the girl to be initiated, has to look submissive. She is not allowed to keep her face upright, since such posture would imply rudeness and bad manners.

The *somo* is usually an elderly woman with child-bearing experience. This is important since she is expected to continue advising the girl throughout her married life on marital, fertility and delivery matters. The *somo* or *mhunga* can only instruct her brothers', sisters' or other relatives' daughters, but never her own. It is taboo to advise your own daughter on such issues. The somo leads the dances and the songs.

The *somo* is generally paid in kind, but sometimes she may receive money. If she is paid in kind, *khangas* are mostly preferred. A *khanga* is a piece of printed cotton cloth worn by women. If the parents cannot afford a *khanga*, chicken and maize flour can be given instead.

Practice of initiation among some matrilineal groups

Most African societies trace their descent patrilineally. Yet, there is a belt of matrilineal societies stretching from east to west, and also from south of the Equator to central Angola and Zambia. The Congo, Zaire, Angola, Zambia and Mozambique largely comprise matrilineal people. Matrilineal pockets are also found in Tanzania (Udvardy, 1988).

Because initiation rites for girls are more elaborate in matrilineal than in patrilineal societies, I visited two matrilineal villages in Morogoro and two in Songea. I also went to two patrilineal villages in Songea. Among the societies I visited were the Yao, the Mwera of Nyasa and Mateka villages in Ruvuma region, and the Luguru of Mtaa wa Pili and Kaole villages in Morogoro region. The main economic activity in these societies is farming.

While authority is vested in the mother's brother, husbands and fathers have little authority over their wives and children (Udvardy, 1988). Thus matrilineal descent does not mean that women have the power to control men in the way that men control women in patrilineal groups. However, a woman has more autonomy and control over her own person than in patrilineal societies. Brothers keep less watch over their sisters' sexual relationships than do husbands and fathers, while it is accepted that any child born to her belongs to her and her relatives, who stand to derive benefit from these children when they grow up (Udvardy, 1988). The same applies in the event of divorce.

For the Yao, the Mwera and the Luguru, a woman is a very significant figure in the family. The residence of spouses is matrilocal. Yet, important rituals, ceremonies and occasions are not allowed to take place until the maternal uncle has given his consent.

The Yao, who came from Mozambique, were allies of Arab slave traders. Although they were influenced by the Islamic religion, their matrilineal clans were not destroyed. Neither did the Islamic religion break the matrilineal structures on the island of Kalpen on the south-western coast of India, according to Dube (1993). I was told by a *somo*, that the Yao referred to their lineages as *mawele* or *milango* (meaning breasts or doorways), and traced them through matrilineal clans. A doorway is a space in a wall where a door opens and closes, and through which a building or a room is entered. The people trace their female ancestors, called *lipata* or *likolo*, as far back as their grandmothers. Their line of descent consists of sisters and their children under the leadership of an elder brother. A man's heir and successor is his eldest sister's son and not his own son or brother.

The Mwera originate in Malawi. They fled the Ngoni raids and settled in Tanzania along the southern shores of Lake Nyasa, hence the name Wamwera, meaning the southern people. Later, some of them went on in search of employment as far as Songea, where they settled.

The Luguru are people who live in the mountains in Morogoro district, hence their name Waluguru, which means people of the mountains. Authority among them is based on matrilineal lineages. Their lineages are ranked for seniority in the following terms, *tombo dikulu, tombo dikati* and *tombo didodo,* meaning large, medium and small breasts respectively. In this respect, their lineages can be traced to the thirteenth or fifteenth generation. It is worth noting that Yao lineages were also referred to as breasts.

The same *mkole* stated that the Luguru originate from different ethnic groups (like Wabunga, Wabena, Wazaramo and Wakutu) of Bantu origin. Their main food crops are cassava, peas, sweet potatoes, pumpkins and vegetables. Only members of the local matrilineage, women as well as men, have rights over the land. Occasionally, the Luguru work on sisal plantations. Divorce is frequent and can be initiated by either spouse. While goods are divided between the spouses upon divorce, the residence site is retained by the woman.

Generally, in matrilineal societies bridewealth is low and divorces are common. A divorce is signified by return of the bridewealth. Thus, in patrilineal societies where bridewealth is higher, divorces tend to be rather rare. This difference also affects sexual mores, since divorced women are likely to have more sexual relationships than married women (Udvardy, 1988).

I also stayed with the patrilineal Ngoni of Songea. They originate from South Africa and came to settle in Songea district in the nineteenth century (Ebner, 1992). I was told that the Ngoni men have marked control over their women and children. The man resides with his wife near his parents' house. The wife has limited influence over her husband and in-laws. The mother-in-law and sisters-in-law exercise authority over her children since they arrange the ceremonies connected with birth, puberty and marriage. They also have to ensure that the children learn socially accepted manners. While the Ngoni mother traditionally was a provider of food, the father concentrated on cash-crop production. In difficult times, the man could count on the support of his brothers who lived in the same neighbourhood. In this way, the male circles were important institutions and had a weighty role in regulating Ngoni family affairs.

This picture corresponds with the general characteristics of patrilineal societies which,

try to ensure that unmarried women's reproductive capacity is preserved for the future husbands' lineages, and that married women's pregnancies are under the control of their husbands' lineages. (Udvardy, 1988:70)

The family patterns in different ethnic groups were influenced by the arrival of missionaries in Tanzania. Among the first to come were the Benedictine fathers who settled around Songea in 1898 (Ebner, 1992). The Ngoni were, therefore, influenced by Christianity. This appears to have contributed to the decline and eventual disappearance of the initiation rite among the Ngoni. However, it is noteworthy that although Morogoro was also among the earliest areas of Roman Catholic missionary endeavour, the initiation rite there has remained intact. It appears that matrilineal groups have been more successful in resisting the impact of patriarchal religions than the patrilineal groups which share similar features of male dominance. Furthermore, female initiation rites are especially significant in matrilineal societies where the girl does not leave her home after marriage (Mead, 1963). The rites also publicly signify that mature young women are available for marriage.

The stages of initiation

In order to understand the current significance of initiation ceremonies, I tried to identify the actors involved and their rules of conduct and to study the observance of these rites and their meanings. In both Ruvuma and Mateka, Kaole and Mtaa wa Pili, groups of girls were initiated during the time of my study.

I learned that in Kaole and Mtaa wa Pili a girl usually passes through at least four stages of initiation. The first takes place just *as she is about to experience menarche.* At about this time she is told by her grandmother or aunt that whenever she sees blood spots on her underwear, she should quickly go back home and remain indoors.

With menarche, she obeys these instructions. At this stage, a bigger ceremony is held and the *mkasone, mkole, mnandi* and *mhunga* become involved. These functionaries mainly comprise close relatives such as aunts and grandmothers but also neighbours and friends. They are assigned special roles to instruct the girl on hygiene, female duties, sexuality and fertility regulation.

Here, the initiation of Beatrice of Mtaa wa Pili serves as an example. She had just reached her menarche. Mama Edna, who, like Beatrice's parents is Christian, was invited to be Beatrice's *mhunga,* i.e., the person who leads the whole ceremony. Mama Edna, therefore, assumed the role of the main instructor. She started by praying that all that would be said would be in accordance with God's will. She continued by explaining the menstrual cycle in layman's language; that it is a sign of fertility and also a blessing from God. She told Beatrice that everybody has "private parts" which are gifts from God. These sacred parts are to be respected and only used with God's permission, that is, only when the girl is legally married. Then Beatrice was made to understand that she was grown up now and that sexual intercourse could result in a baby in nine months' time. She was told that the main method of avoiding pregnancy was abstinence. She was strongly urged to control her sexual urges and advised to keep herself busy with work if she felt the need for a man. A good girl is expected to marry and only to bear children after marriage. Beatrice was also given instructions on her female duties and discouraged from playing childish games.

The send-off ceremony is held on the eve of the wedding. This ceremony is well organized in Ruvuma and Mateka as well. The *mhunga* plays a significant role in instructing the bride on how to handle her husband, and repeats what the bride needs to remember as a wife. This can be done through story telling and singing. Stories and songs have hidden meanings and are easily memorized. The following were sung during initiation in Ruvuma and Mateka:

– Achapi mwele, achapi mwele
kutia pasi kusikia kunuka

(There was a girl who never properly washed
her sanitary towels,
When she ironed them, the smell was foul.)

Chorus: Toka toka toka toka mshenzi we malabuku we
Mwanamke gani ah
Hujui kupika ah
Ukipika wali ah
Unakuwa mbichi ah
Ukipika mchicha ah
Unatia mchanga ah
ukilala kitandani ah
kama sindano na uzi ah.

(A girl who is very lazy
and does not know how to cook,
neither has any sexual skills
when it comes to a closer look.)

– Zuhura nipele mwana wane
Nipagate Ali mwiganga, nipagate Ali mwiganga.

(Zuhura, I want you to bear a child for me.
Why can't you?)

The girls are also told that it is very important to wash the wooden spoon and the cooking pot immediately after having cooked *ugali*, stiff porridge. This is a metaphor for the girl's cleanliness or dirtiness after sexual intercourse. The wooden spoon is a symbol of the penis and the cooking pot of the vagina. The initiates are expected to interpret and internalize this message.

During the send-off ceremony of Joha of Ruvuma village, instructions about sexual intercourse were given. The main counsel of her aunts centred on how she should handle her husband during the sexual act since she would soon be married. During the counselling, the aunts were dancing and singing special songs which conveyed particular messages to the bride. Occasionally, they demonstrated sexual intercourse by twisting their waists. This was meant to show Joha the skills that she could apply to her husband. On this occasion, the *somo* acted as a leader by initiating the songs and dances. The main purpose of the ceremony was to ensure that the girl would be able to satisfy her husband-to-be. If the wife fails to perform satisfactorily during intercourse with her husband, the somo will be blamed. At worst, the girl could be rejected by means of divorce.

However, the initiation ceremony is also an institution for enforcing values. It is a socially approved way to emphasize gender and, especially the qualities of a good wife. All this was demonstrated during Joha's send-off ceremony when the presentation of gifts to the bride took place. Special messages from her parents and close relatives, as they gave her cash presents, advised her on how to live with her husband, in-laws and other relatives. Then came the turn of the invited guests. Their presents included cash, kitchen utensils, various pieces of equipment, mats, wooden spoons, baskets and *khangas*. *Khangas* with special messages were preferred. Joha's parents gave her a pair of *khangas* with the printed message "*Wazazi tumeridhika mkae pamoja*" ("the parents are happy for the couple to be married"); a friend presented a *khanga* with the caption "*Mke mwema ni taa ya nyumbani*" ("a good wife shines at home"); and yet another had the text "*Uchawi wa mke ni ulimi wake*" ("a woman's power lies in her tongue"). The messages underscore what is hoped for and feared from a wife.

Joha's *somo* is not the only one who gives her protection. She will also be supported by her peers with whom she can share her experiences and problems. However, the *somo* is expected to continue advising Joha on procreation and sexual matters throughout her married life. It is her *somo* who will advise her on safe delivery, the appropriate time for weaning her baby and the time for conceiving again.

When a girl is *about to have her first child* the *mhunga* and *mkasano* give her advice on safe motherhood and delivery.

After her child is born, she is taught to abstain from sexual intercourse for two years, in order to protect her baby from being harmed by the semen which is believed to poison her milk. At this stage, the wife might move to her parents or in-laws for at least three months. The girl is advised not to be jealous when her husband turns to other women. This method of spacing encourages polygamy. The young mother risks getting inadequate attention from her husband. The *mhunga* added that the wife was assured proper care by her parents or in-laws. However, nowadays, due to economic hardships, the mothers may not be able to take care of their daughters and their babies. Also, women were traditionally producers of food. Currently they tend to produce cash crops and neglect food crops. Yet the cash received is not sufficient for the mother herself, her daughter and the grandchild.

The cases of Beatrice and Joha of Ruvuma illustrate the significance of initiation in providing girls with protection from, or at least warnings about, the dangers associated with puberty, and in advising them about how to satisfy their husbands-to-be.

The ceremony also offers a way for girls to gain confidence as grown-ups. The young woman is assumed to become knowledgeable about the nature of sexual desire and her ability to conceive. She will be able to pass on such information to others. In addition, the initiation ceremony is a way of announcing that initiates are ready for marriage.

Laws of conduct

The initiation ceremony has its laws of conduct. In Ruvuma and Mateka areas, in Kaole and Mtaa wa Pili, the initiation ceremonies take place simultaneously for girls and boys. The ceremonies are usually arranged during school vacations so as to allow the novices to prepare themselves, to live in seclusion, to go to the forest and to be released. Only elders who have passed through the rites themselves may perform the girls' initiation rites. They are usually members of the adolescents' extended family, excluding their parents. All novices must be of the same sex – it is prohibited for one gender to witness the ceremony of the other gender.

The ceremony has different actors including the hosts, who are the parents of the girl to be initiated. Their main role is to make sure that there is plenty of food and beer for the whole ceremony. The maternal uncle is expected to contribute a large amount of food or money. The embrace of the ceremony will very much depend on the availability of food and beer. These items will also determine the length of the seclusion period. If the parents and uncles are wealthy, the girls may be secluded for a longer period, even for more than a month.

The family's prestige and cohesion are demonstrated during the initiation rites. The participants consume a lot of food and beer. Domestic chores are carried out collectively. People dance and exchange gifts. Those who attend other people's ceremonies and present gifts, expect a big attendance and many presents at the time of their own daughter's initiation.

The ceremony of Saviana serves to illustrate the prestige involved. Saviana was thirteen at her menarche. Her parents are poor peasants from Mateka. To supplement their meagre income they occasionally work for rich farmers. In order to make their daughter's ceremony successful, they had to cultivate five acres of cassava for a payment of 4,000 shillings, and purchase thirty kilograms of maize meal plus five kilograms of meat. The money and supplies were used to entertain guests during the three days of ceremony before the girl was secluded. During seclusion, the girl had to stay inside and was not allowed to show herself to the public *(kumweka ndani)*. Close relatives contributed with beer and other supplies to make the occasion successful, and to show their cohesion. The father, Mzee Geugeu, and the mother had to work again for the same rich farmers to earn another 3,000 shillings and purchased thirty kilograms of maize meal, and five kilograms of meat for the ceremony of releasing the girl *(kumtoa mwali)*. This occasion signifies the end of seclusion. Mama Maria, Saviana's sister, was among the people who gave her presents. She gave Saviana a pair of shoes and some *khanga*. Mama Maria earned the money for these items by cultivating the field of another rich peasant.

The relatives and other guests included grandmothers, aunts and female cousins who had already passed through the ceremony. A paternal aunt is considered to have special influence on fertility, and she is expected to be influential in shaping the girl's behaviour. If the girl has bad manners, the paternal aunts are blamed.

The ceremony itself involves many activities; beer, feasting and dancing. During the first three days, dances are held at the novice's home during the day and at night. Before the novice is released, she is sent to the forest and stays there for three to five days.

In African allegories the bush and the village are often opposites, the bush signifying sorcery and clandestine action. It is a domain of dangerous powers and wild energies, while the village stands for social order, community and collective responsibility. Thus, the bush is inimical to the social order. But it also stands for the generative powers of persons as individual agents. Going to the forest (or bush) symbolizes the need to create "some kind of balance between the vital but unruly energies associated with the bush and the orderly world of the village". Thus it is "a refraction of a deeper need to adjust individual freedom to its limiting conditions". (Jackson and Karp 1990:19)

The wild sources of fertility have to be domesticated for an ordered social world. The gap between the established order and the world of unconscious individual experience has to be bridged. Or, expressed differently, the impulses of the bush have to be adjusted to the imperatives of the village (Jackson and Karp, 1990). The anthrophologists interpret the bush as a symbol of the power of individual will and intelligence without which the collectivity would cease to exist.

While in the forest, the novices wear a piece of cloth up to their waists and leave their breasts bare. They are taught many things, stories are told and songs with hidden meanings are sung. If a girl has bad manners, she is punished; she is pinched and warned to leave her rude manners behind and mend her ways. The novices are not allowed to take a bath while in the forest. When they return home, they are again secluded until the day of release *(siku ya kutoka)*.

The day of release is a very cheerful one, a day of triumph. Now it is time for the novices to take a bath and then appear in their best clothes. The occasion is marked by beer and food feasting and the candidates are presented with various gifts. Many words are uttered in praise of the girls and the initiation ceremony is concluded.

The initiation of Saviana also demonstrates some of the rules of conduct in the ceremonial process. When Saviana was secluded, nobody except the *somo*, her mother and sister were allowed to speak to her. The *somo* was the only woman permitted to be with Saviana during the first three days of seclusion. On the third day, the

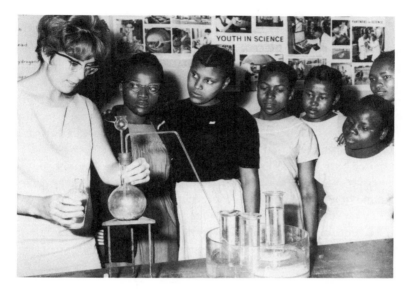

They no longer "cover the cup", but learn scientific experiments.
Maelezo, Dar es Salaam

ceremony of seclusion was completed and people could leave and resume their daily work. However, Saviana remained indoors for a whole month, as she was not allowed to be seen outside the house.

During the seclusion, the *somo*, mother and sisters were not permitted to speak to other elderly people, neither women nor men. In fact, they avoided any form of contact with the elders. They wore strings made from local herbs around their necks as protection against evil spirits and to preserve Saviana's fertility. It is believed that some people, especially older men and women, have evil eyes which can cause barrenness among initiated girls. Caution is needed because elders are less fertile, and talking to them will reduce the young woman's fertility. The strings around the neck remind the *somo*, the sisters and the mother that they have to abstain from interacting with barren old people.

Covering the pot

In Ruvuma, Mateka, Kaole and Mtaa wa Pili it was revealed that people knew about child spacing and fertility regulation and that they used several methods to achieve it. There are two main methods, one being those natural ones which do not involve use of man-made devices. The most commonly used is abstinence. Others are *coitus interruptus* (withdrawal before ejaculation) and safe periods. The man-made methods include putting a piece of cloth in the vagina before sexual intercourse and the oral consumption of traditional herbs. Other methods are inspired by supernatural beliefs and include tying a string around the waist, wearing a talisman, or the ritual covering of a pot for the whole period of desired barrenness. When the woman wishes to conceive, she simply uncovers the pot. These man-made devices are mostly used by truant unmarried girls who want to prevent pregnancy before marriage. They mostly obtain this knowledge from their grandmothers.

According to cultural anthropologists (Jacobson-Widding and van Beek, 1990), the clay pots are associated with female fertility in agricultural societies all over sub-Saharan Africa. Thus, in the strongly matrilineal societies of Central Africa this leitmotif is explicitly displayed during fertility rituals. The art of making pots constitutes the crucial feature of initiation rites.

That the female womb is symbolized by a clay pot is apparent, and not only in the matrilineal cultures of Central Africa. For instance, the Shona of Zimbabwe use the clay pot to symbolize the bride's womb at a particular moment in connection with the conclusion of the marriage contract. After having checked her virginity, her paternal aunt gives her a clay pot filled to the brim with water. If she is a virgin, the bride should hand over this pot to her husband, without spilling any water. If she is not a virgin though, she is supposed to spill out some water from the pot before presenting it to her husband...Being a crucial metaphor of the creative power of the adult woman, the clay pot may also feature as a fundamental symbol of female identity and the sense of worth accompanying a clearly established identity. (Jacobson-Widding and Van Beek, 1990:25)

I must admit that, like most educated people in my society, I have not really been aware of the cosmologies and symbols of fertility in African cultures. In fact, it is only in connection with my study that

I have learned about matri – and patrilineal patterns and the rich cultural meanings behind the customs and symbols.

Initiation ceremonies are still important stages in defining womanhood in the matrilineal societies I visited. Yet, I became increasingly conscious of the inadequacy of traditional institutions in today's society, and so far no proper replacements have evolved.

In Peramiho and Maposeni, where the patrilineal initiation rites have withered away, the girls do not receive any systematic instruction from their relatives; they just acquire bits of information from their peers and mates. As such, they run the risk of being misinformed. Traditionally, grandparents and aunts were responsible for organizing initiation ceremonies, although these were never as elaborate as those of the Yao and Mwera.

I also noticed that the aunts and grandmothers in Peramiho and Maposeni now seldom give any proper fertility instruction. Since it is taboo for mothers to talk about sexuality to their children, the girls have no reliable person to turn to. For that matter, the community is losing its role in organizing collective initiation ceremonies. For example, during the interviews I learned that Peramiho and Maposeni girls had heard about traditional methods of fertility regulation from their friends or schoolmates, although they deny using them. Most of them also agree that they are familiar with modern contraceptives. They admit to using them and state that they got the information from maternal and child health clinics and the mass media. The school system and mass media are somehow trying to address this problem.

Opinions differed as to the effectiveness of the traditional methods of fertility regulation. Some girls from Ruvuma and Mateka villages, where initiation rites are still practised, have been using traditional methods. They have used strings and oral herbs but were uncertain about whether the methods worked or not. However, Paulina Chemba, a traditional birth attendant, knew about various local contraceptives. In her opinion, they are reliable, since her customers have used the methods and they have worked. Her customers include both married and unmarried girls. Fatu Mwinga, a traditional herbalist of Dar es Salaam, also asserted the usefulness of local herbs for fertility control.

In Morogoro and Songea, I encountered mixed feelings on the

effectiveness of traditional methods. There was an interesting story told by a girl called Ancilla Makuana from Kaole village. This girl got married when she was fifteen years old and gave birth to her first born at sixteen. A year later she had twins. She and her husband agreed not to have any more children, at least not within the next two years. They went to see Ancilla's grandmother, who referred them to a medicine man. He gave Ancilla a string to tie around her waist and after that she did not conceive for four months. Then she missed her period for one month, and thereafter experienced irregular menstrual flows. When she saw the medicine man again, he told her not to worry as she was not pregnant. Yet, the problem persisted and Ancilla was examined by a gynaecologist from a government hospital. It was found that she was pregnant and she later delivered healthy twins, a boy and a girl.

I also had the chance to meet two women who relied on traditional knowledge. Etropia Mkoba is the second wife of the ten-cell leader and a mother of two. She admitted to knowledge of various bush roots which are used as contraceptives. She is one of the few women who knew and had experience of these medicines. She had used them before she got married and they worked. According to her, married women use these control devices very rarely because most of them would like to please their husbands by bearing as many children as they can. The users of these medicines are, therefore, unmarried girls who want to prevent pregnancies before marriage.

Tausi Rashidi is also married and she has a child. She indicated that her grandmother had provided her with some oral roots and strings. She had used them for one year and four months and had not fallen pregnant. Her husband has travelled to Dar es Salaam to look for employment. She used the traditional methods to escape the consequences of her extramarital affairs.

According to the information I gathered, it is apparent that premarital adolescent pregnancies are fairly common. In fact, I found that most girls give birth before marriage. They face considerable difficulties, and this is equally true of the matrilineal Ruvuma and Mateka girls, and the patrilineal Perahimo and Maposeni girls. The young mothers received little or no economic support from their partners, let alone their parents and in-laws.

For example, Binti had her menarche at thirteen. An initiation ceremony was held for her. Her aunt, grandmother and other elderly women taught her about hygiene, sexuality, menstruation and conception. She was also instructed on her female duties such as cooking, taking care of children, submission and good manners. Yet, she was left with abstinence as the only way to prevent pregnancy.

Binti was fourteen and had just completed her Standard 7, when she met a driver. He took her to a guesthouse where they had sexual intercourse. The man gave her 500 shillings and that was the last she saw of him. She soon realized that she was pregnant. She went to see her aunt who broke the news to her parents. The father got very angry. He expelled both the girl and her mother from the house. They took refuge at their neighbour's house, where they stayed for two weeks. The neighbour pleaded on their behalf and the father accepted them back. Throughout her pregnancy the father never spoke to Binti and she received no support from him.

After Binti had given birth, her grandmother showed her how to take care of the child. She urged Binti to abstain from sexual intercourse in order not to harm the child. After a year, the grandmother tied a string around Binti's waist to prevent her from conceiving. She also prepared a medicine to prevent the baby from being harmed. She had observed that Binti had started to go out with men again. Binti conceived again, but luckily, this time the man who impregnated her took care of her and the children, although he has no intention of marrying her.

How to fill the gap?

In the early days, abstinence was usually not a problem. One *mkunga* of Mtaa wa Pili explained to me that girls were traditionally instructed at puberty on the meaning and practice of sexuality. At the same time, it was insisted that they should abstain from sex. Virginity and its preservation was one of the measures of compliance. If the girls were still virgins at their wedding they were rewarded, but if not, some of the bridewealth paid for them was returned to the groom's parents.

Sexual intercourse before marriage was discouraged. In those days, girls would be married from the age of fifteen. This was generally not more than a year after menarche. To abstain from sexual intercourse during the short period between puberty and marriage was, therefore, not seen as a problem. Abstinence was also practised when a wife had had a child to prevent her from conceiving again too soon. In extramarital relationships, man-made contraceptives were apparent, especially if the husband was away for a long time. These were also used if the woman could not resist her husband's sexual demands while the baby was still small.

Nowadays, the interval between puberty and marriage is getting longer and longer. This is because girls are preoccupied with many activities, including schooling and economic pursuits, which make them delay marriage. During the course of my study, I gained the impression that initiation is nowadays failing to accommodate new social needs, thus making it ineffective. Research findings, for example, revealed that initiation ceremonies offer contradictory instructions: on the one hand, they provide instructions on sexuality and, on the other, they insist on abstinence. In the villages, I met girls who were about to marry. They marry from the age of seventeen. Abstinence for more than two years after puberty is becoming a problem, especially as girls now interact more freely in mixed groups and take part in social gatherings.

In Peramiho, for instance, it is not unusual to find girls being entertained in *ulanzi* bars equipped with discos. *Ulanzi* is a bamboo wine common in southern Tanzania. The girls will be invited for drinks. An increasing number of girls use their bodies to earn money and, therefore, fall pregnant. This situation was also demonstrated among Ruvuma and Mateka girls who have a high rate of pregnancy before marriage despite the persistence of initiation rites.

From the interviews at Songea Girls Secondary School, it was revealed that the biology of reproduction is being taught in schools. This is a clear indication of how modernization has removed sexuality and reproductive health from its socio-cultural context and the realm of traditional society and placed it in the school curriculum. It is my view that this type of education leaves the gaps unfilled because social expectations and the range of information imparted at the initiation ceremonies about sexuality and reproductive health are not covered by the curriculum. It also emerged that instructions given through the mass media do not embody social values.

Initiation ceremonies could become more effective if they readdress themselves to current issues. Fatu Mwinga's experience is a case in point. Fatu Mwinga is a traditional herbalist who has her own clinic for treating patients with various diseases. Among other things, she is engaged in research on various herbs which can be used as medicines and traditional contraceptives.

Fatu established an *unyago* club after she had done some research and collected data from various ethnic groups on the need for, and the need to improve, initiation for girls. Parents with daughters who have had their menarche go to register at the club. When the group is large enough, a date is set and members of the club, including the mothers, are invited to attend the ceremony. Each girl is instructed in accordance with her traditions and customs. Usually, members of a club will include some members from the girls' respective ethnic groups, and these people will lead the ceremony. Only those who have themselves passed through initiation in their adolescence can attend as members.

According to Fatu, the main functions of her *unyago* club are to teach girls at puberty or brides-to-be, as well as women with various problems related to reproductive health. These instructions include the function of the woman's body, especially the reproductive organs. They also include the meaning of puberty in relation to reproduction, and various social and cultural taboos related to sexuality. The girls are also taught good manners, what the society expects of them, self-reliance and self-development in order to satisfy their economic needs. Moreover, they are taught birth control by various means, such as abstinence and modern as well as traditional contraception. They are also cautioned on their side effects. However, instruction of contraception depends on the wishes of the parents.

Fatu has seen the need to incorporate new areas of social concern in her work. Among these are AIDS and its effects, how to handle AIDS patients, and the need to avoid as well as possible ways of preventing the disease. For her, the current problem is not only pregnancy out of wedlock, but also the deadly HIV virus and other current social and economic problems.

Traditionally, initiation was a link between puberty and marriage, and a demonstration of women's roles. The ceremony at puberty was essentially meant to prepare the girls for marriage. My study shows how modernization has taken instructions on sexuality out of their social and cultural context. The rites which were organized at community level are becoming more individual and private. The modern approach is biomedical and puts less emphasis on the socio-cultural meanings of sexuality and fertility. In the past, the rites of transition aimed at protecting the moral and reproductive order in the context of given societies. At present, the community allows its daughters to fall into the breach between tradition and modernity.

References

American Friends Service Committee, 1970, *Friends Society of Who shall Live*. Report prepared for American Friends Service Committee. New York: Hall & Wang.

Biesans, J. and M. Biesans, 1971, *Introduction to Sociology*. USA: Prentice Hall Inc.

Cory, H., 1956, *African Figurines. Their Cermonial Use in Puberty Rites in Tanganyika*. New York: Grove Press.

Dube, Leela, 1993, "Who Gains from Matriliny? Men, Women and Change in a Lakshadweep Island". Paper presented at conference on Changing Gender and Kinship in sub-Saharan Africa and South Asia, University of Nairobi.

Ebner, Fr. Elezear, 1972, *The History of Wangoni, Peramiho*. Ndanda: Benedictine Publishers.

Goody, J., 1976, *Production and Reproduction: a Comparative Study of Domestic Domain*. London, New York, Cambridge: Cambridge University Press.

Hill, R., 1979, *Family and Population Control*. Chapel Hill: The University of North Carolina Press.

Hines, W.E., 1963, *Medical History of Contraception*. New York: Gamat Press Inc.

Jackson, Michael, and Ivan Karp, 1990, *Personhood and Agency: The Experience of Self and Other in African Cultures.* Uppsala Studies on Cultural Anthropology 14. Stockholm: Almqvist &Wiksell International.

Jacobson-Widding, Anita, and Walter van Beek, 1990, *The Creative Communion: African Folk Models of Fertility and the Regeneration of Life.* Uppsala Studies in Cultural Anthropology 15. Stockholm: Almqvist & Wiksell International.

Mamdani, M., 1973, *The Myth of Population Control, Family Caste and Class in an Indian Village.* New York: Monthly Review Press.

Mbunda, M.W., 1989, *Adolescent Fertility in Tanzania, Knowledge, Perception and Practice.* Dar es Salaam: UMATI.

Molnos, A., 1968, *Attitudes Towards Family Planning in East Africa.* München: Weltforum Verlag.

Molnos, A., 1973, *Cultural Source Materials for Population Planning in East Africa. Beliefs and Practices.* Nairobi: East Africa Publishing House.

Omari, C.K., 1980, *Some Aspects of Family Planning in African Society: The Tanzania Case.* Dar es Salaam: Department of Sociology, University of Dar es Salaam.

Rigby, P., 1963, *Cattle and Kinship among the Gogo.* London: Cornell University Press.

Southall, A.N., 1960, "On Chastity in Africa", *Uganda Journal,* 24.

Stycos, J.M., 1964, *Control of Human Fertility.* New York: Cornell University Press.

Udvardy, M., 1988, *Social and Cultural Dimensions for Research on Sexual Behaviour,* Society and HIV/AIDS, Department of International Health Care Research, Karolinska institutet.

Vuyk, T., 1991, *Children of one Womb.* Leiden: Centre of Non-Western Studies.

Wilson, M., 1957, *Ritual of Kinship among Nyakyusa.* London: Oxford University Press.

6. The case of the matrilineal Mwera of Lindi

Mary Shuma

It has recently been reported that Lindi rural district ranks second in the country for high mortality rates among children and pregnant women (Daily News, 4 June 1993). In 1985, the mortality rate for children under five was the highest in the country, with 236 out of 1,000, compared to 191 out of 1,000 countrywide (1988 Census). Lindi is reported to be one of the leading regions for school drop-outs due to pregnancy. At the same time, girls and boys are still undergoing traditional initiation rites. I was curious to know more about the initiation rites and the early pregnancies. In order to explore the situation, I chose an ethnic group, the Mwera in Lindi, as the target for my study.

Lindi region is in the southern part of Tanzania. It has a total population of 646,550, which is 2.8 per cent of the nation's population (1988 Census). It is one of the most sparsely populated regions with only ten people per square kilometre as compared to, for example, eighty-three for Kilimanjaro and eighty-six people for Mwanza.

The land of the Mwera of Lindi lies between nine and ten degrees south latitude. It is a low-lying stretch of land with the highest hill not more than sixteen hundred feet. To the north of it is Matandu River while the southern part borders the Makonde escarpment. Rainfall is very unreliable and the rivers flowing through this area dry up during the dry season. People, therefore, depend on waterholes for their normal supply of water.

I visited the Mwera for a month in 1991 and learned about their customs and living conditions. A retired local teacher told me about the origins of the Mwera. The Mwera are a Bantu ethnic group with their cradle in the northern part of Uganda near Lake Albert. They settled on the eastern shore of Lake Nyasa. Slowly the group divided itself in two groups – one is now living beside Lake Nyasa in Ruvuma region and is known as the Mweras of Nyasa. The second group moved to Mafia Island near Kilwa, settled there and gradually expanded along the Indian Ocean coastal strip to the present Lindi and Nachingwea districts. They are called the coastal Mwera, while the group discussed in my study are referred to as the Mwera of Lindi.

"Mwera" is a word which simply means "those living in the mainland (Kumwera), far from the coast". Apparently those who lived on the coast looked down upon those inland, and, therefore, called them Wamwera, which simply means mainlanders. The Mwera are generally known to be very peaceful. While travelling from the coast inland, the Mwera of Lindi met enemies who seized their belongings and killed many of them. Many others died while trying to escape and some starved to death. This meant a tremendous reduction in their numbers.

At present the Mwera of Lindi live in small oval shaped huts mostly thatched with grass. When constructing them, the men look for building poles, women fetch thatching grass and young boys dig the clay used to make mud for the walls. These people work in groups and they work on one family house before moving on to another. By tradition there are certain tree species which may not be used for building houses. A reason for this ban is the belief that a "ghost" would haunt such a hut. This apparently protects those tree species from extinction.

The Mwera of Lindi keep no domestic animals such as cattle as the area is infested with tsetse flies. They get most of their meat from hunting and they also fish. Nowadays, the mission centres have piggeries which provide the people with pork.

The Mwera are mainly subsistence farmers with a comparatively low annual per capita income of less than US$ 30.00 as compared to the national average of more than US$ 50.00 (1992 prices) (National Accounts of Tanzania, 1976–92). Their main food items are millet, rice, maize, groundnuts and vegetables. The area around Rondo Plateau is famous for hardwood (*mninga*) which is used for construction, but is more widely known from the Makonde carvings, a form of art and handicraft highly appreciated by tourists.

Cashew is the main cash crop. Over the years cashew production has fallen drastically and this has led to the closure of some of the factories which used to employ a significant number of people. This decline can be attributed to poor soils, unreliable rains, as well as the villagers' lack of interest in caring for the trees given that the price offered by the government for cashews is considered unattractive. Moreover, the level of the infrastructural development is generally low. The roads are not maintained and in very poor condition. They are passable only during the dry season. It is thus difficult to reach the rural areas where most of the crop is produced. This partly explains the apathy about deteriorating production that is displayed by both the people and the government. Many people do not opt to work in the Lindi region because of its isolation. Most schools are run without enough teachers and enough qualified teachers, and hospitals and clinics in the region are run without enough doctors and nurses.

The conflict between initiation and education

While I was in Lindi I had discussions with people who were closely concerned with the issue of teenage pregnancy, including the teenage mothers themselves, parents, community leaders, medical personnel, teachers, religious leaders and court officials. Thus, I talked to insiders as well as outsiders within the community, i.e., those who are Mweras themselves, and those who originate in other regions and have been appointed to offices in Lindi. All these people gave their full support to the study. This was more than I had expected. The positive reaction may have been due to the fact that many recognize the problem, and that this was the first attempt to study it in order to assess its magnitude and implications. It was, however, easier for me to follow the arguments of the educated outsiders who held office in Lindi, than it was for me to fully grasp how the local Mwera looked upon themselves and the meaning of their family relationships.

For somebody like me, who was born and brought up in a patrilineal society in Kilimanjaro region, where the education system was largely influenced by missionaries, it was difficult to comprehend the matrilineal rules. My society is fairly rich but very strict in the upbringing of its daughters. Traditionally, it was taboo for a young, unmarried Chagga girl to become pregnant. Such a girl would be punished by the community even to the extent of being tortured to death in one area of Chaggaland. Initiation rites are no longer practised. These days, although the society is still strict and looks down upon unmarried young girls who fall pregnant, at least parents will often do all they can to get their daughters back to school or to give them the necessary assistance if they should drop out of school because of pregnancy.

Among the Mwera, both boys and girls go through traditional initiation rites called *likomanga* and *chikwembo* respectively. This is an important aspect of their upbringing which moulds their cultural identities as women and men. While boys are initiated at a place far away from their homes, mostly in a forest or the bush, girls are initiated in the home of a person to be chosen by their relatives and in a shelter called a *chiputu*. *Chiputu* is a temporary shelter for the girl initiates that is made of branches of a special fast-growing tree. This tree is used to symbolize the obligation of the children who have slept in such a shelter to bring forth children as soon as possible – such are the expectations of initiation. In most cases, girls are initiated by an elderly woman (*kungwi*) of the community. In the early days, boys and girls in this ethnic group went through initiation rites at the age of twelve and above, after which they were expected to get married. There were no pregnancies out of wedlock, because there would be no time for a girl to deliver before she got married. In most cases, girls and boys were initiated after the parents had already earmarked a partner for marriage. In the past, a girl, therefore, was married immediately or shortly after initiation.

Now things have changed. Modernization requires children to pass through the formal school system and, since school attendance is mandatory in Tanzania, the pupils in Lindi face a completely new situation.

The Ministry of Education outlined a policy of Universal Primary Education (UPE) in 1977, requiring each child of school age (seven years and above) to be at school; and his/her education has to continue uninterrupted. Because education is free, a pupil is expected to go through the seven years of primary education without interruption. The policy stipulates that any person who interferes with a child's education will be brought before a court of law. Despite this, and given the social emphasis on traditional initiation rites for children, the community in Lindi initially continued to initiate its children when they reached puberty. However, this meant that the pupils had to be taken out of school for one or two months. This being against the ministry's directive, the parents were taken to task for interfering with their children's education. One of the parents, Saidi, narrated how he was imprisoned with hard labour for six months for taking his daughter (or possibly niece), Salama, out of school for two months for initiation rites.

I will never forget the experience in prison, and I curse the head-teacher for having reported my case, which I still see as no issue. These children have to be initiated in order to be accepted as true members of our society any way.

This man went on to explain how the elders had convened a meeting to discuss how to reconcile the state's claims with those of the traditional culture. At that meeting, the elders decided to avoid conflict with the modern education system by lowering the initiation age to seven years instead of twelve and above. From now on, the children were to be initiated just before starting Primary One, and the parents would not need to take them out of school for puberty rites anymore. It is important to note here that for the Mweras traditions are as important as modernization, and they have tried to find means of reconciling local and national institutions. In this particular case, they merely changed the age of initiation, but not the objectives or the content of the rites. But while traditional initiation had been meant to prepare young people for marriage shortly after initiation, with the lowering of age to seven years, initiates will instead start school.

According to my informant, Mama Nachinga, initiation includes instruction on how a boy or a girl should deal with his or her partner in intercourse, and also how a woman should give sexual satisfaction to a man. The girls are trained in a technique which requires them to lie on their backs, while a woman sits on her or something heavy is put on her waist. The girl is then asked to move her waist rhythmically while the heavy object is on her. This weight represents the man, who, it is assumed, will lie on the girl during sexual intercourse. The girl continues this exercise until she has acquired the skill of moving her waist while there is a heavy load on her. From demonstrations that I observed, I admit that this technique needs practice before it can be mastered. In earlier days, the initiated were expected to practise these skills frequently among themselves as they grew up. I was told by Mama Nachinga that the messages of sexuality and marriage once imparted to pubertal youths have remained largely unaltered in spite of the lower age of the novices. Put differently, the message now has a double meaning: just wait until you are old enough, but do not lose your skills.

As a result, boys and girls go on proving their sexual powers, and these early sexual encounters give rise to teenage pregnancies. These, in turn, lead to their expulsion or their dropping out from school.

Gloomy prospects for the future

The Mwera girls who had been expelled from school because of pregnancy considered my study as their salvation. Their responses and narratives indicated a state of despair with regard to the future. Parents and community leaders seemed concerned about the increasing numbers of children born out of wedlock and the future that awaited them. Doctors were worried about the rate at which young girls were dying because of complications during pregnancy. Girls as young as thirteen years are advised to give birth in hospital where there are better facilities. However, very few girls are able to make the journey to the government hospital in Lindi town. The community I studied is ninety miles from Lindi and public transport is rarely available. Most expectant mothers in this locality, including the young girls, therefore deliver at home with the assistance of traditional birth attendants. These attendants are unable to handle severe cases of excessive bleeding, obstructed labour, hypertension or eclampsia, with the result that many such deliveries end fatally. In addition, the young expectant mothers are themselves malnourished owing to the poor harvests and the low income of their families, and they bring forth malnourished children who often do not survive. This explains the relatively low rate of population increase in Lindi, 2.0 as compared to the national increase of 2.8.

In one of the localities, I came across Mariana, aged thirteen. She was pregnant. Mariana confirmed that she had had no previous experience of menarche. This means that she became pregnant during her first ovulation. Mariana was made pregnant by a boy of her peer group and she conceived as a result of sheer sexual experimentation. I wanted to know where and how she had met the boy.

Mariana explained that the boy was her age-mate, a neighbour who had attended initiation rites at the same time as she had done. They met for intercourse in either the boy's or her family's premises, apparently with the knowledge and tacit approval of the parents. They considered this conduct as proof that initiation had had the required effect and that their children were becoming adults. The Mwera do not consider it bad for a young unmarried girl to fall pregnant. She is not expected to abort or abandon her child and she is not harassed by her mother, her maternal uncle or her father. Indeed, her pregnancy is considered a credit to the girl, because it is proof that she is fertile and capable of bearing children. Girls are born to bear children. Never mind about age. As soon as a girl is capable of conceiving, she is ready to bear a child, is how Hamis, a village elder, described the situation to me.

In Mwera culture, the attributes of a prospective wife include being able to cook stiff porridge properly (*ugali*), and to take good care of the kitchen utensils. It is also desirable for a woman not to have stiff breasts (Mwambe, 1970). Any young girl who is not sexually active is supposed to have stiff breasts. One has to be sexually active or deliver a baby and breast-feed it in order to lose the the stiffness of the breasts. A prospective wife among the Mwera, therefore, is expected to be sexually active or to have had a baby and to have breast-fed it, if Peter Mwambe is correct.

Another girl I came to know was Aisha, a girl of fourteen. She had been expelled from school because of pregnancy. Nassoro, who made her pregnant, happened to be her classmate. When talking about their relationship and the time when she and Nassoro were having sexual intercourse, Aisha admitted that she had received petty things, like an exercise book, a pen and pocket money for school trips. Apparently, Nassoro raised such money by travelling long distances after school hours in search of water, firewood and thatching grass which he sold to the villagers. Now Nassoro had also been expelled from school and both came to discuss the matter with me in the hope that they could be assisted back to school, at least for their final primary school examination which was due in a month's time. Although I felt sympathy for Aisha and Nassoro and wanted to help them, there was not much I could do, because the law does not make exceptions, even for pupils with good past records.

I was especially concerned about Aisha because she looked pale and malnourished. Recalling what the medical personnel in the area had told me about survival chances for girls in her condition, I was scared that Aisha was going to die in labour. I had long discussions with her about her well-being, but she resisted my recommendations about nutritious foods like eggs and vegetables. According to her, it was taboo for an expectant Mwera mother to eat such food. My anxiety led me to keep contact with Aisha and her mother. Fortunately, Aisha survived during delivery but not the baby. She is still asking for my assistance because Nassoro is nowhere to be traced in the village.

Caught between two forces

One must stress the fact that girls brought up in a culture with traditional initiation rites experience a period of confusion both around and within themselves. They are clearly caught between two forces. On the one hand, there is the national policy that seeks to improve girls' opportunities for formal education. On the other, there are the immediate pressures exerted by the family and by custom. One also needs to recognize that schools are often not able to deliver on the promise of education. The head-teachers of the schools were concerned about the unavailability of competent teachers and the resultant poor performance of pupils. Consequently, only a few pupils continue on to secondary school after their primary education. According to head-teachers, this situation discourages parents from ensuring that their children attend school. The parents would rather have their children concentrate on other cultural matters, like the traditional initiation rite that is a basic requirement of full membership of the Mwera community.

Where both the demands of education and cultural woman- and

manhood exist simultaneously, one of the forces will lose and give way to the other. So far, many girls have been more responsive to community pressure and have thus fallen pregnant and have had to give up school.

Further investigation of the cultural messages concerning the regeneration of life revealed that no information on conception is communicated to the girls. According to the girls, they were told during the last days of initiation that "you have grown up" (*umekua*), which could be interpreted to mean that the girls were ready for adult roles. The girls did not seem to have any idea that pregnancy is the result of coital experience. On the one hand, ignorance of conception could be linked to the whole idea behind these traditional initiation rites which requires sexual practice in order to retain the skills one has learnt. On the other hand, ignorance about conception could stem from the observed Mwera belief that knowledge about conception and birth should never be communicated to children. Traditionally, children were told that babies came from the sea, a tale that persists. As a result, girls engage in sexual intercourse heedless and ignorant of the consequences.

The matrilineal system of the Mwera

It was evident that young teenage mothers take custody of their children with the help of relatives, mainly mothers and maternal uncles. The Mwera of Lindi are a matrilineal society in which marriage entails the husband's movement to the wife's premises.

The children are named after the woman's brother, the maternal uncle. He is responsible for important rituals and ceremonies. Such occasions must not take place until the maternal uncle has been informed and has given his consent. The maternal uncle brings up his sisters' children. The bridewealth is also handed to him when his sisters' daughters get married. As such, some uncles are reluctant to ensure that the girls complete their schooling. After the girl has been initiated, the uncle will be more interested in securing her marriage for the sake of prestige and bridewealth.

My own cultural background repeatedly prevented me from grasping the social logic of the matrilineal society, particularly the significance of the bond between sister and brother, and the lesser importance given to the marital relationship.

I had to recognize that the kind of concentration of control that a patrilineal father or husband enjoys over property and women's sexuality and reproductive power is simply not available to matrilineally related kin. I had to accept the idea that in matrilineal societies, authority is very often diffused and is not concentrated in a single individual or in men. It had never occurred to me that the patrilineal system functioned at the expense of women, that women's membership of their natal groups is peripheral, that they are transferred to their husband's groups where they long remain outsiders or suspect and that they have a purely instrumental value as bearers of children for the paternal line. I did not realize that in a patrilineal system the absence of rights over property makes women vulnerable to different kinds of oppression. The opposition between outsider and insider; the tensions involved in the girl's socialization, which emphasizes control over her sexuality; the asymmetry between brother and sister and between husband and wife; the internalization of an ideology that circumscribes and devalues women, are all linked to patrilineal systems (Dube, 1993). I had never thought of it in that way. Instead I looked upon matrilineal systems as primitive and poor, so poor that the men had no economic power to command over women.

I got upset when I found that the Mwera boys who impregnated girls did not support them materially, or financially. In my opinion, this premise perpetuates the cycle of teenage pregnancies and early motherhood. The boy does not bear any of the consequences of his actions as he is not obliged to care for the child or the girl. He can fool around with as many girls as he likes, producing children and forgetting about them. No legal action is taken against boys who make girls pregnant, although the law provides for that. Yet, girls, on the other hand, do not necessarily shoulder the burden either, since their maternal relatives take over the responsibility of raising the babies. Consequently, the girls can go on falling pregnant and bringing forth children.

It took me some time to grasp that husband and wife can be separate entities, that a married wife does not lose her rights over her person and that a child belongs to its mother and her matrilineal group. The fact that a father has little authority over his children and traditionally has no legal responsibility for their maintenance also baffled me. However, not all matrilineal systems are identical, so it is necessary to examine again what else is expected of a father.

Among the Mwera, most of the girls' relatives live at subsistence level. As a result of this poverty cycle, many girls are themselves malnourished. The malnourished girls bring forth malnourished children who often do not survive. Sometimes, the young mothers themselves do not survive either. This explains the relatively small size of the households, on average only 4.6 as compared to the national average of 5.2 (1988 Census).

The situation is made worse by the belief of these young girls' mothers that their daughters die because of witchcraft (*uchawi*) and not because of pregnancy complications. The mothers do not, therefore, see the relationship between death and juvenile pregnancies. Furthermore, these mothers have had a different experience of life. Marriage after initiation was the obvious course and marriages were more permanent then than they are at present. Still, matrilineal societies do not place heavy emphasis on marriage. Marriages may be casual. Social stability is associated with the maternal line. Although many marriages end in divorce, the bond between sisters and brothers remains intact.

The meaning of marriage varies. The Mwera used to have a custom that men booked pregnancies to secure future marriage partners or male companions. If the baby to be born happens to be a girl, she automatically becomes the wife of the man who booked that pregnancy. In such a case, the man may decide to take his wife, the small girl, at any time he wishes. I found young Neema, eight years old, living with her future husband's mother. The husband's maternal family had financed Neema's initiation ceremonies and they assured me that Neema would live with them until the husband-to-be marries her. I doubted that the son was going to wait for Neema to complete the seven years of primary education, especially when she lived in the same household. If, on the other hand, the baby to be born is a boy, then he remains a good friend of the man who has booked that pregnancy. In other words, the relationship is like that between a father and son in many matrilineal groups. After having learned more about preferential marriages among matrilineal people (Vuyk, 1991), things started to make sense to me.

Traditional beliefs and practices among the Mwera are even stronger than religious ones. Initiatives taken by the Catholic church to reduce teenage pregnancies in the locality are an indication of this. The church organized traditional initiation rites for girls to be conducted in church in the hope of injecting some religious aspects into the programme, especially with regard to premarital sexual practices. The effort failed, according to the priest, because the church could not attract participation in the programme. People felt that the programme was rather contrived, and that children would not learn from it. They, therefore, opted for a traditional way of initiating their children.

When I look at matrilineal descent and initiation rites among the Mwera, I am disturbed. I acknowledge that it is difficult for me to suppress my patrilineal bias. Beyond that, however, it appears to me that men are taking advantage of customs and traditions which have been degraded by modernity, and that the victims of such conduct are mainly children and mothers, in this case teenage mothers. The girls fall pregnant while very young and only a few get married. Too many of them face an early maternal death, too many lose their children.

A pattern of casual sexual life is dangerous in view of the spread of sexually transmitted diseases like AIDS. Although AIDS was not prevalent in this area during the course of this study, it is easy to foresee its emergence, not least because the current distribution of AIDS roughly corresponds to the distribution of matrilineal societies, although it also embraces people of indigenous patrilineal descent around Lake Victoria. The latter area has, however, had a history of social upheaval over the past twenty years. So far, Lindi district has been protected by its isolation. The Lindi-Kibiti-Dar es Salaam highway, currently under construction, will create a new situation when completed. My worries about the future vulnerability of the Mwera women are shared by local medical personnel.

There are many questions that I cannot answer yet. However, I will revisit Mwera to clear my mind about matriliny and the Mwera concept of marriage and to sort out the outsiders' and insiders' views of the Mwera moral order. Thus equipped, I will involve myself in discussing how to influence Mwera customs so as to protect the people from becoming victims of AIDS.

References

Bureau of Statistics, 1992, *1988 Population Census: Basic Demographic and Socio-Economic Characteristics*. Dar es Salaam: Planning Commission.

Bureau of Statistics, 1992, *1988 Population Census: Infant and Child Mortality. Regional and District Estimates*. Dar es Salaam: Planning Commission.

Bureau of Statistics, 1993, *National Accounts of Tanzania 1976–1992*. Dar es Salaam: Planning Commission.

Daily News, 4 June 1993. Dar es Salaam.

Dube, Leela, 1993, "Who Gains from Matriliny? Men, Women and Change in a Lakshadweep Island". Paper presented at conference on Changing Gender and Kinship in sub-Saharan Africa and South Asia, Univiversity of Nairobi.

Mwambe, Peter, 1970, *Wamwera na Desturi Zao*. Ndanda: Mission Press.

Udvardy, Monica, 1988, *Social and Cultural Dimensions for Research on Sexual Behaviour*, Society and HIV/AIDS, Department of International Health Care Research, Karolinska institutet.

7. Looking for men

Betty Komba-Malekela and Rita Liljeström

In the past there was no dating in the sense we understand it today. In many tribes, such practices were unthinkable. Girls were married off when they were very young or upon reaching puberty. Many things have changed. How are the relationships established today between teenage girls and their boy-friends? Who are they? Where do they meet? What do they expect from each other? Betty Komba-Malekela went on to find answers to these questions. She wanted to explore what goes on in the urban context: how do the girls relate to men?; what kind of patterns emerge in towns where social control is weaker than in rural areas? Rita Liljeström has added her comments – trying to interpret some of the findings.

Teenage girls in urban centres

To find answers to such questions, I interviewed eighty girls aged between fourteen and nineteen years. Half of them are from Dar es Salaam, and twenty from the Mbeya and Ruruma regions respectively. They all come from varied urban localities, ranging from an affluent ward inhabited by office executives, big businessmen and traders in the capital to a semi-squatter area in Mbeya town, where people survive by means of petty trading in foodstuffs and second-hand clothes.

How did I get in touch with the girls?

At the grassroots level in Tanzania, ten houses constitute a cell under the ten-cell leader, in Kiswahili known as *Mjumbe wa nyumba kumi.* Once I had reached a site, I introduced myself to the *Mjumbe*, explained the purpose of my study and sought his help to identify teenagers in the locality. I then approached the girls and explained the purpose of my visit. About 80 per cent of them were willing to answer my questions.

More than half of the girls had primary education, although eight had dropped out of primary school. Nearly one-third of the girls were in secondary school, but only one girl had completed Form 6. The rest had completed their education in the period between 1987 and 1992.

The largest group among the girls were schoolgirls or students and the second largest group were the unemployed as can be seen from the ranking of their employment status:

schoolgirls, students	23
unemployed	13
business/petty business	9
agriculture/livestock	7
housemaid/housewife	6
pre-school teacher	5
hotel waitress	4
clerk, typist	3

Other occupations mentioned were dress- and embroidery makers, tobacco worker, nurse, hotel manager, UMATI agent, etc.

Most of the girls' parents have primary education. Very few of the mothers or fathers have secondary education. As evidenced in many other studies, the fathers have more years of formal education than the mothers. This is also true of the girls and their boy-friends.

Regarding the occupations of the girls' parents, I found that at least half of the mothers were either housewives or busy with agriculture. Even in cities, people still depend on agriculture as an occupation or to augment their incomes. Families normally own gardens or *shambas* (farming land) on the outskirts of the cities. Twelve mothers had jobs in sales or as clerks.

A large proportion of the fathers were engaged in jobs other than farming: business and petty business, professions, crafts, technical and mechanical jobs, etc. Except for agriculture, they had similar occupations to their daughters' boy-friends.

Two-thirds of the parents were staying together while a third were either widowed – five fathers were dead and one father was unknown – separated or divorced.

Who are their boy-friends?

While all the women interviewed are teenagers, the bulk of them being in their upper teens (17–19 years), *the ages of the men* they are dating vary from sixteen to forty-two years as can be seen below.

Table 16. *The ages of the boy-friends*

	Dar es Salaam	Regional towns	
20 years or younger (16–20 years)	16	9	= 25
men in their thirties (21–28 years)	12	18	= 30
at least ten years older than the girl (26–42 years)	12	13	= 25
Total	40	40	= 80

Most of the men in the youngest group in Dar es Salaam were secondary school boys or students having girl-friends with a similar status.

A majority of the boy-friends have primary and secondary education. A few have further education. It is assumed that men normally prefer women who are on par or who have lower educational levels.

Since the cities and locations visited were quite different socially and economically, the men's occupations were also diverse. The most common occupations among the boy-friends were:

businessman	19
petty business	4
pupil, student	12
clerk, banking	6
driver	4
techn. mechanics	4
police	3
medical assistant	3
teacher	3

Other occupations mentioned were factoring, manager, warder, tailor, carpenter, electrician, farmer, construction worker, bus conductor, guest-house manager, bar manager, doctor, nurse. Only two men were unemployed.

A quarter of the men are married and have family responsibilities. These men tend to belong to the oldest group among the boy-friends. The remaining three-quarters are single men who are looking for a wife. For a man who is single and has a job, it is common to have three or four girl-friends. The teenage girls I interviewed complained about the fact that their boy-friends have several girl-friends. Thus, "having a boy-friend" often means sharing a boy-friend with a couple of other women.

A few married men were looking for additional wives. One of them had recently married a sixteen year old housemaid. She said that she was happy to become his second wife. Two other girls told me that their boy-friends intended to marry them as their second and third wives respectively.

Some of the married men were twice as old as their girl-friends and economically well off. No doubt, they have the upper hand, especially as half of the girls were unemployed or made their living in petty business or agriculture. Other girls had jobs and could at least make a living. In a few cases, the girl and the married man were employed in the same shop, office or school, although at different occupational levels.

One can hardly blame the men for the girls' dependency on them given that many girls prefer men who can afford to spend money.

Where do they meet?

Contacts between women and men in urban environments assume that money is being spent. Often, if not always, it is the men who have to spend their money, not only to entertain their girl-friends, but also to buy them presents, such as dresses, wristwatches, earrings and shoes. This was not the case in rural areas in the past, but has become increasingly true even there.

The girls and the men meet in buses, at work-places, in schools and churches, at the market or when window shopping. They make acquaintance at dance, music and cinema halls. Some of them live in the same neighbourhood. Young women and men meet casually, without having made any plans or appointments. However, they know where the opportunities are good to meet the opposite sex. An exception is Mbinga town, where contacts between girls and men still take place during traditional *lindeku* dances. While girls in Dar es Salaam meet their boy-friends in public, in Mbeya town, Tukuyu, Songea and Mbinga it is not common to see school-girls loitering with boys in the streets.

In an economically well-off district in Dar es Salaam the teenage girls were knowledgeable about modern social activities like going to the cinema, going to dances or watching videos and television during weekends. This is much less true of the small regional towns.

It all begins when a girl and a man become attracted to one another. They engage in petty talk. After having established contact and having started a relationship, they are tense and excited about the partner. The men offer lifts and buy snacks for the girls. They also give them different kinds of nice things.

It used to be men who approached women rather than the other way around. Most men would be surprised if the woman took initiative, particularly if she is a teenage girl. According to what the girls told me, the pattern is changing. A majority of the girls I interviewed maintained that they themselves had chosen their boy-friends. They do it by flirting with their eyes, by swaying their hips

They make acquaintance at dance and cinema halls.
Photo: Trond Isaksen, Bazaar Bildbyrå, Stockholm

when walking near the men or by giving them food, like rolls and buns (*chapati and maandazi*). In more urbanized areas, the girls display their interest, while in the smaller towns, more girls admitted that they had been selected by the men or that friends had selected boy-friends for them. However, who is choosing whom is an intricate issue. The girls may have liked boy-friend long before they were approached by him. When the opportunity arose, they just agreed, thus conforming to their hearts' desire. In this sense, they had chosen the boy-friends.

Boy-friends pick up some of the girls, while other girls find boy-friends through relatives or friends. It is rare for parents to encourage such a relationship, unless they are assured of a possible marriage. However, in some cases, poor parents may expect their daughters to come home with money or presents which can help the family to make ends meet.

The lovers' gifts

Teenagers need education, clothing and shelter. Those who live in good and modern houses feel proud of this fact and aspire to nice things. The girls like the latest fashions in clothes. Hence, the girls I met preferred boy-friends with steady and high incomes. At first glance, it does not make any difference whether they belong to a poor or rich family. And yet it does, since some teenage girls have boy-friends in order to get their daily bread, while others seek drinks, fashionable clothes and nice things.

The socio-economic status of the boy-friend seems to afford security to the girls. Seemingly, among many of the respondents I interviewed, good education, and a stable and reliable income stand out as basic requirements. About half of the girls expect love and sex from their boy-friends. Some of them also expect drinks and money. Only one out of five girls cited hopes for the future. They hope to have a child and to get married.

When I asked the girls if they had sex with their boy-friends, most of them admitted they did. The data suggest that it is rare for a man to associate with a young woman just for the sake of companionship. Only a few, mainly students, were not having a sexual relationship. Otherwise, there were no indications of any differences between teenage girls from different family backgrounds with regard to having boy-friends. Initially, however, sex might not be explicit. Rather, it occurs after repeated requests. Given the expenses that are often incurred by boy-friends over a given period, the inevitable question arises as to how to repay these expenses. In general, teenage girls eventually succumb to the men's sexual advances. Many of them meet at their boy-friends homes, because it is more difficult for them to meet at their own homes where their parents mostly are very strict. The couples also go to hotels and guest houses. Few parents are aware that their teenage daughters are having affairs. And very few of the girls know about modern contraceptives and have access to them.

Even though the teenage girls and their male friends become associated with varying motives, generally the girls gain financially from the men. Four out of five girls interviewed admitted that they received money from their boy-friends. Since girls often have boy-friends not because they like or love them, but mainly for money, a saying has arisen in Dar es Salaam, *"Hapendi mtu bali pochi"*, literally meaning "no money, no love". Material benefits are one of the incentives for the relationship, while sheer love or the expectation of marriage is often of secondary importance or none at all.

Salana, a young girl from Tunduru, had migrated to urban Songea. After her arrival, she stayed with her sister who was employed as a housegirl. So they worked together in the same household. Since her sister had a boy-friend, Salana decided to obtain one as well. To this end, her sister talked to a certain man who was eager to have a girl-friend.

Salana told me that she enjoyed the relationship. Sometimes the man gave her 2,000 shillings per night, sometimes she only got about 500. However, the amount she received was relatively generous compared to what she had received from her boyfriend in Tunduru. She looked very young and tiny and she had no plans to marry. She preferred it the way it was.

Some girls go out with men frequently. Patricia, eighteen years old, explains:

Every day there is a man coming to pick me up. There are several of them. You know, I am unemployed and I have nobody to depend on. These boy-friends buy my meals and other things that I need.

Patricia has no plans to marry. She has boy-friends in order to make ends meet. She assured me that she uses condoms to protect herself against AIDS.

Likewise, there are men who have girl-friends, not necessarily for the purpose of marriage, but just for fun. They enjoy the company of young girls who are dubbed *dogo dogo* which literally means "small small" and has the same connotation as "spring chicken". It is not unusual to see married and respectable aged men dating girls, some of whom are of their daughters' age.

Twenty out of the eighty teenage girls interviewed admitted that they had become pregnant. Yet only fourteen of the girls had a child. Twelve of them were born out of wedlock. Thus, it is evident that the girls either have had miscarriages or abortions.

Miriam, from Temeke district, confided to me that she was in love with a man. They were business partners and had had a child together, but at the time I saw her there was no suggestion of marriage. She lived in fear that her boy-friend might abandon their son.

In addition to the risk of pregnancies out of wedlock, teenage girls run several other risks in their relationships. Nearly a quarter (nineteen) of the girls have contracted venereal diseases, and thirteen out of eighty reported having been beaten. Some boy-friends are very jealous. They do not like their girl-friends to talk to other men, even relatives, work-mates or neighbours, or being absent on their arrival home. The men then think that the girl must be with another man. Consequently, these girls are being roughed up and often for nothing.

Ngonyani had a girl-friend who had a boy-friend. Thus she decided to have one too. She used to visit a boy and eventually they became friends. Their relationship went on for two years. However, the boy-friend never mentioned anything about marriage. Ngonyani started to look for other men in order to find someone who would marry her. Unfortunately, one day her former boy-friend met her with another man. She was badly beaten by him. Ngonyani told me that she was just trying to find someone who would say that he liked her and wanted to marry her. Many town girls end up having children out of wedlock because of their anxiety to get married.

However, nearly half of the teenage girls do not perceive problems in their relationships with their boy-friends.

Asked what they think about women who earn their living by prostitution, all of the girls interviewed expressed negative attitudes. Prostitution as a way of life has not been socially accepted although both men and women are involved in the exchange of sexual services and gifts. Still, prostitution as an occupation is abhorred.

When I asked the teenage girls about their futures, three out of four said that they preferred to be full-time housewives. Engagement in agriculture was their second best option for the future.

Images of "African sexuality"

In the past, the clan monitored the behaviour of its youth. At present, different ethnic groups mix in the towns. Intermarriage creates confusion. Somehow, the couples have to sort out their different customs and values.

Girls as well as men get hurt when they realize that their motives and expectations are different. Young women hurt men by their desire to obtain money and gifts instead of appreciating the man himself. Men hurt young women by harassing them for sexual intercourse without mentioning marriage. There is a lot of bitterness and many misconceptions between the teenage girls and the men.

In spite of disappointments, at least half of the interviewed girls feel that their boy-friends have a positive attitude towards them. However, only a few of the men had mentioned any plans for marriage although thirteen men expected to have a child from the relationship. About a quarter of the girls think that their boy-friends' attitudes towards them are negative or that they are only interested in sex.

How do these findings correspond with what is known from other sources?

Two main images of "African sexuality" appear to exist. Both assume that it is permissive and promiscuous. One emphasizes the instrumental and commercialized character of the extensive sexual exchanges taking place, especially in urban environments. The other image dwells on the remnants from the past and their impact on values and attitudes today. What would a short-hand description of these two positions highlight?

Some researchers have simply explained the permissive and promiscuous features as a continuity from a tribal past where sexuality was never inhibited by religion and moral considerations (Caldwell *et al.*, 1989), while others (Ahlberg, 1993) see them as resulting from the erosion of an old reproductive and moral order which did, indeed, regulate sexuality. These regulations varied and could be very strict, although they often differed from similar rules in Eurasian societies. Colonialism, missionaries, labour migration, urbanization and other modernizing influences have dissolved the old controls and undermined much of the meaning that sexuality had in tribal cultures.

The instrumental view

For decades already, the offering and expectation of sexual services has been pictured as a routine part of city life in Africa, comparable to the taking of bribes (Little, 1973).

Multiple studies from several sub-Saharan countries repeat the same stories of the men's sexual appetites and the women's instrumental approach in extracting money and gifts for sexual services (Standing and Kisekka, 1989) and the establishment of sexual patron and client relationships. Standing and Kisekka's bibliography on sexual behaviour in sub-Saharan Africa contains several entries on the socio-economic context of "sexual instrumentality". Part of that context is the absence of labour-market opportunities for women which forces them into certain niches.

The towns provided a chance to amass some independent income from trading, beer brewing and the provision of urban-specific services and from the sale or exchange of sexual services. For some women in towns, therefore, casual and informal serial relationships with men provided a more viable or attractive alternative to marriage. This continues to be the case for some sections of the female population in urban Africa and this suggests that it is important to understand the structural antecedents of what appears at first sight to be an increase in "promiscuity" in towns. (Nuffield workshop, 1988:73)

Obbo's case study (1987) of elite marriages in East Africa during the 1970s sheds light on relationships between elite married men and women in modest white- and blue-collar jobs. For such women, liaisons with elite men were one of the few paths to improved financial security. For the men these women, generally found at the work-place, formed a convenient pool of sexual opportunity, less risky than the alternative pool of bar hostesses and night-club girls when it comes to contracting sexually transmitted diseases. The women provided domestic services as well.

Also Mandeville (1979) found that the main support for female lovers comes from married men with a high status and to a lesser extent from single men who are postponing marriage. According to her,

securing a paying lover may be indispensable to a woman who wishes to live and bring up children in town, and the practice may tell us more about her wish to educate her children, or her dislike for rural life, than it does about her sexual or marital preferences. (Mandeville, 1979)

Like many other researchers, Obbo (1980) stresses the high level of sexual antagonism which characterizes gender relations, and the serious need of women for the security that an income brings. Salaried women are to a high degree exposed to sexual harassment, especially when job promotion is involved. Obbo claims that her data from Ugandan urban areas are representative of gender struggles in other African cities.

Stichter (1985) who has written on migrant labourers, notes that "all personal relationships between men and women inevitably become colored by the inequities of differential relations to the capitalist labour market" (Stichter, 1985).

Standing and Kisekka confirm that the instrumentalist understanding of sexual exchange appears widely in the literature on urban Africa. They call for studies that examine the male point of view.

Male potency as a bond with ancestors

At the core of traditional culture stood the cult of fertility and the regeneration of life. Religion and belief are pervaded by sexual symbolism. Anita Jacobson-Widding studies the Shona people of Zimbabwe. Her observations are valid for many Bantu people south of the Equator and to the west of the lake district. She is one of the few anthropologists who has focused on sexuality. The following description comes from personal communications between her and Rita Liljeström.

Sexuality is the focus of rain ceremonies, as well as views of life and death. While female sexuality is surrounded by ambivalence, men are expected to be active sexually for as long as they live.
Daily News, Dar es Salaam

Sexuality stands as the focus of rain ceremonies as well as of views on life and death. While female sexuality is surrounded by ambiguities, and menarche and menopause mark the beginning and the end of a woman's sexual life, men are expected to be sexually active as long as they live. If not, they are excluded from eternal life. The prerequisite for life after death is potency. A man has to be potent when he dies, otherwise he cannot become an ancestor who "rains" his semen to fertilize the soil. Rain ceremonies aim at exciting the male ancestors to release their "rain".

The phallocentric worldview is reflected in the symbolic language of daily talk, in architecture and the use of tools for preparing food and cultivating land. This culture of fertility is partially explicit, partially implicit. Among people who live in the modern sector it tends to be implicit. But the basic message remains the same: men must constantly prove their potency, whether they have access to their wives or not.

The men's value as human beings depends on the proof of their permanent potency. The issue is not to prove potency to others, but to oneself, for one's own personal worth and for one's "eternal worth".

According to Jacobson-Widding, unwanted pregnancies as well as sexually transmitted diseases among young women in urban centres in Africa cannot be seen apart from the male potency fixation. The problem has deep existential roots and probably goes back to experiences in early childhood. Recent articles written by African men (Tuguta, 1994; Masanja and Urassa, 1994) endorse her evidence by describing how even small boys are constantly observed to see if they react normally to sexual stimulation, and how men who are not able to produce offspring face a tragedy of cosmic dimensions.

This image of African sexuality makes possible the interpretation of findings that are otherwise difficult to grasp, such as the intentions of the thirteen men who wished to impregnate their teenage girl-friends without having any intention of marrying them. It also fits with Obbo's (1987) discussion of the ideologies of sexuality.

...Female sexuality is inextricably linked to fertility and...East African men of all classes and backgrounds require proof of a

woman's fertility. This often accounts for premarital pregnancies among young girls and women, as they either yield to male pressure or else use pregnancy in order to maintain a partner. (p. 80)

Not only do studies indicate that premarital relationships not infrequently result in pregnancy, but also that multiple relationships are fairly common which means that young men may make more than one girl pregnant. The men emerge as strongly pro-natal. (Jahoda, 1973. Chaplin 1973)

Also, the habit of single men to have three or four girl-friends simultaneously can be seen as an effort to prove male potency and thus self-worth. What is tragic is that men prove their worth at the expense of women, and thus contribute to the persistence of distrust between the genders. Many urban men have their families elsewhere. According to Jacobson-Widding, the dissemination of AIDS has evoked the fear of death, or to be more precise, the fear of not having an eternal life. Therefore, the man has to continue to prove his potency until the very end, even if tests have shown that he is contaminated with HIV.

In sub-Saharan Africa, married couples did not form a unit in the same sense as Eurasian families did. The boundaries between different categories of kin were clearly marked in clan societies. The same applies to the boundaries between clans, generations and other categories. No boundaries were more sharply drawn than those between women and men. The two genders lived and live in separate spheres. They do not work together. They do not spend their leisure time together. They do not share meals. They do not take a bath or wash themselves in the presence of one another. The only thing a woman and a man have in common is the night, says Jacobson-Widding.

In this context, the relationship between husband and wife is full of contradictions. They share the intimacy of sexual intercourse, yet they are kept apart during the day, not least symbolically. They do not talk about sex, they cannot go to the river to take a bath together before the woman has reached her menopause. In the past, these boundaries made it possible to avoid physical intimacy and the dangerous mixing of bodily fluids. However, they prevented the two spheres from overlapping and kept women and men alien to each other. Remnants of this alienation can be traced in the current antagonism between men and women.

References

Ahlberg, Beth Maina, 1993, "Is there a distinct African Sexuality?" Dept. of International Health Care Research (IHCAR), Karolinska Institute, Stockholm, and Dept. of Sociology, Uppsala University.

Caldwell J.C., P. Caldwell and P. Quiggin, June 1989, "The social contex of AIDS in Sub-Saharan Africa", *Population and Development Review*, 15, 2.

Jacobson-Widding, Anita, 1991, *Personal communication*.

Standing, Hillary, and Mere N. Kisekka, 1989, *Sexual Behaviour in Sub-Saharan Africa – A Review and Annotated Bibliography*. Prepared for the Overseas Development Administration, London.

Tuguta, M.Y., 1994, "A Participatory Exposition of Attitudes, Behaviour and Practices influencing Reproduction and Family Size Choice among the Wakerewe, Tanzania", *in The Challenge of Complexity*. Third World Perspectives on Population Research. The Swedish Agency for Research Cooperation with Developing Countries (SAREC), Stockholm.

From Standing and Kisekka has the following references been taken as secondary sources:

Chaplin, J.H., 1973, *Wiving and Thriving in Northern Rhodesia*, C.M. Turnbull (ed.), *Africa and Change*. New York: Knopf.

Jahoda, Gustav, 1973, "Love, Marriage and Social Change: Letters to the Advice Column of a West African Newspaper", C.M. Turnbull (ed.), *Africa and Change*, New York: Knopf.

Little, K., 1973, *African Women in Towns. Cambridge*: Cambridge University Press.

Mandeville, E., 1979, "Poverty, Work and the Financing of Single Women in Kampala", in *Africa*, 49, 1, 42–52.

Obbo, Christine, 1980, *African Women: Their struggle for Economic Independence.* London: Zed Press.

Obbo, Christine, 1987, "The Old and the New in East African Elite Marriages", D. Parkin and D. Nyamwaya (eds.), *Transformations of African Marriage.* Manchester University Press/International Africa Institute.

Sticher, Sharon, 1985, *Migrant Laborers.* Cambridge: Cambridge University Press.

Whitehead, Ann, and Megan Vaughan, 1988, (eds.), Nuffield College workshop papers on "The Crisis over Marriage in Colonial Africa". Nuffield College, Oxford

8. Too little too late

Zubeida Tumbo-Masabo

My study was initiated on the assumption that most teenage mothers have their babies before they are fully aware of their reproductive capabilities. The problem is worsened by the fact that many teenage girls fall pregnant out of wedlock and are afraid to approach their parents and other relatives for any help regarding childbirth and their responsibilities thereafter. I was curious to find out how teenage mothers got to know about sexuality and childbirth. This concern arose from my own experience of having my first child in 1974. When I was six months' pregnant, my mother, who is a midwife, gave me a midwifery textbook to read (Myles, 1971). The book, which was in English, gave details about labour management. However, when the day of labour arrived, I had forgotten everything. Furthermore, when I made contact with the midwife at the hospital, I could not understand the Kiswahili terms that she was using and, hence, I had difficulty in trying to communicate with her, a difficulty, I suppose, that she was also experiencing.

Only some teenage mothers are fortunate enough to attend antenatal clinics which mainly monitor their health but do little to teach them about childbirth. It is either taken for granted that the girl knows about the subject or that it is the duty of someone else to teach her about it.

Others are able to attend prenatal initiation ceremonies whereby they are taught, usually in less than a day, about childbirth, but are given no chance to ask for clarification or elaboration. Any questions from the girl are usually interpreted as a sign of rudeness or knowing too much. A girl is not supposed to display her knowledge of sexuality and childbirth. Asking questions is taken by many adults as a sign of showing off rather than as an indication of ignorance. Hence, the girl is left with many unanswered questions.

I wanted to find out about the type of knowledge that teenage mothers have about sexuality and childbirth and the methods that they use to acquire that knowledge. Since there are very few materials on how teenagers learn about sexuality and reproductive health in Tanzania, I tried to capture the self-image and the knowledge that teenage mothers have in their own words.

Since the words and terms that are used in a community are crucial for effective communication, I also scrutinized the use and definitions of some common Kiswahili terms that are utilized to define processes pertaining to the body, sexuality and childbirth. I decided to use Kiswahili because it is the most widely spoken language in Tanzania. Consequently, the study was conducted in areas where I could get a substantial number of mother-tongue Kiswahili speakers, i.e., in Dar es Salaam and Ujiji.

Dar es Salaam was chosen because, as a cosmopolitan city, most of its residents are fluent in Kiswahili, the major *lingua franca* of the city. Besides, for the young generation which has been born and reared in the city, Kiswahili is sometimes the only language that they know (Polomé, 1967).

Ujiji has long been an entrepôt for the caravan trade (Tippu Tip, 1966) and has remained an important centre in the trade between Tanzania, Zaire, Rwanda and Burundi. Kiswahili has been a significant *lingua franca* or first language for many for a number of centuries, both during the caravan trade era and after. I decided to concentrate on two of the main actors during pregnancy and delivery, the teenage mothers and the midwives, and to learn of their experiences of the matters at hand by interviewing them.

Teenage mothers I talked to

Forty teenage mothers participated in the study; twenty from each area. I found the first teenage mothers variously through a friend, a relative or a colleague, as I could not use formal channels of administration to identify them. The first young mother then led me to another in the neighbourhood or to somebody who had attended the same clinic or with whom she had been together at childbirth. The other teenage mothers acted in the same manner until the required number was reached.

The teenage mothers were divided by age at first childbirth: 14–17 years (juniors) and 18–19 years (seniors). However, to maintain consistency, I decided to interview only those girls with one experience of childbirth. Also, due to difficulties in recalling the experience with the passage of time, I interviewed only those girls who had given birth within the last five years.

Almost all the teenage mothers had finished seven years of primary education before falling pregnant. In Dar es Salaam, two girls fell pregnant when they were in the first year of secondary school and three during the sixth and seventh years of primary education. Hence, differences in responses due to educational levels were negligible.

Twenty-four of the teenage mothers were unmarried. Nineteen of them came from Dar es Salaam.

While all the married teenage mothers were interviewed at their homes, the unmarried ones did not feel comfortable about talking to me near members of their families, fearing that their fathers would come in during the interviews. The main reason for the fear was that they did not want to create the impression that they enjoyed being single mothers.

In most communities in Tanzania, as with many communities in the United States of America (Phoenix, 1991: 20), sexual activity among *unmarried* teenagers is considered unacceptable. Hence, the unmarried teenage mothers I interviewed wanted to show that they regretted their "unacceptable" or "immoral" conduct by not allowing me to interview them in front of their fathers and other elderly male relatives. The need to conform to the norm has affected not only the girls themselves, but is also reinforced by male-biased research. As Mbilinyi (1984:289) puts it:

Anthropological analyses of the social structure of family and kinship described the subordinate position of women, but ignored all signs of rebellion and resistance. A false picture of the timid, shy acquiescent African woman was presented by the African male chiefs and elders, and happily reproduced by European social scientists. It fits their own image of ideal female behaviour, and reflected the direction which the colonial state (as well as the independent government) was taking in regulating male–female social relations.

In spite of the reservations families have about out-of-wedlock pregnancies, mothers and close female relatives felt the need to teach teenage mothers about child-bearing despite their marital status. Hence, the methods used and the knowledge gained showed no distinct variations as between married and unmarried teenage mothers.

Experiences on menarche and childbirth

I asked the teenage mothers to narrate their own experiences of and feelings about menarche and childbirth. They were later asked to explain some Kiswahili reproductive terms.

One Kiswahili book I found which discusses the reproductive health of women in detail is that by Dr. Kaisi (1976). The book, which is a teaching manual for rural midwives, starts with a brief discussion of infections related to reproduction, followed by a description of the female genitalia.

The book makes use of common Kiswahili terms, for example:

kuvunja ungo	menarche
hedhi	period
mimba	pregnancy
mji wa mimba	uterus
nyonga	pelvis
kondo	placenta
kitovu	umbilicus
chupa	amniotic membranes

These terms were familiar to almost all the teenage mothers that I interviewed. However, the author errs in the use of particle *ya* when he uses the term kondo *ya nyuma* (afterbirth) (Kaisi, 1976:24). Most of the teenage mothers who participated in the study were familiar with the more commonly used kondo la nyuma.

It was almost impossible to get any book which elaborated on sexuality, and Kiswahili terms that are used to explain it were not easily found. Therefore, there is a need to try and explain sexuality.

The social construction of sexuality

The explanation of sexuality in sub-Saharan Africa, and, for that
matter, in Tanzania, is not easily accomplished. As a lexicographer
by profession, I consulted the *Unabridged Random House Dictionary*
(RHD) of 1987, and found that it defines sexuality as (p. 1755):

1. sexual character; possession of the structural and functional traits
   of sex
2. recognition of or emphasis upon sexual matters
3. involvement in sexual activity
4. organism's preparedness for engaging in sexual activity.

How do possession of traits, recognition of matters, involvement
in activity, and organism's preparedness fit into African realities?
They are all abstract and empty concepts, devoid of social and
cultural meanings, as if sexuality were something "objective" and
simply given by nature, and not socially constructed and imbued
with meaning.

Some intellectuals have explained sexuality as "heterosexual and
homosexual intercourse, child sexuality, sexual pleasure in different
erogenous zones of the body and not restricted to the male female
sexual organs" (Mbilinyi, 1985:112). This implies a broad knowledge
and appreciation of one's body and bodily pleasures beyond the
heterosexual intercourse which has sometimes been erroneously
viewed as the sole sphere of sexuality. However, here I look upon
sexuality in the context of heterosexual intercourse.

Neither does this second definition take account of social
construction which is so important in dealing with sexuality. Even
pleasures and passions, desires and emotions, taboos and guilt,
sensual and lubricious qualities, are mediated and appropriated
through cultural interpretations. Also, sexual relationships rest on
systems of descent and rules that regulate conduct. Thus, the social
construction of sexuality in itself covers a complex and
multidimensional field. Beyond that, the cultures of sexuality in
Africa have undergone transformations that make them extremely
difficult to pin down, and that is not my aim. I just want to make a
few general remarks on sexuality in sub-Saharan Africa.

ВИА 85-N0012 (5)
Gardez ceci
bien en vue *
ne demande
nouvveau votre
ticket

Please keep
in view so that
not be distur
for your ticket

Date

Call Place

VIA

ıality in most African cultures was open. A free expression
ılity does not mean that sexual activity is not regulated. Sex
ıce within strict rules of conduct, being part of the moral
Ahlberg, 1991, 1993). What Ahlberg reports about the
is not unique to them. Because of the strong belief in the
tween conduct and community well-being, individuals were
· to breach the socially accepted code of conduct. However,
ұthen these codes, taboos, prohibitions and social sanctions
:ensively used. In addition, the society was organized in ways
ıimized the violation of rules.
ıewly initiated men and women were, for example, allowed
together and to practise a form of controlled sex without
ion in order to achieve sexual satisfaction. Since premarital
ırse was prohibited, sleeping together required strong
ıe. Such discipline did not develop naturally, but was in-
uring a long process of education and maintained by peer-
ressure.

In most precolonial sub-Saharan societies, fertility regulation
has been an integral part of the social and economic system. To
ensure proper childspacing, people commonly practised sexual
abstinence after about the fifth month of pregnancy, and during
lactation which lasted two to three years. During this time, the
husband had access to other women. Groups of elderly women took
steps to ensure that the lactating mother did not engage in sexual
intercourse with her husband, or with other men, in order to protect
the well-being of the baby (Ahlberg, 1991).

In the historical encounter between Africa and the West, the
sexual patterns of Africa were grossly misunderstood, and many
assumptions about them were incorrect. Missionaries and colonial
administrators were not able to understand customs that were alien
to their own cultural background, such as polygamy, female
circumcision, ritual sexual intercourse, or the fact that women and
men could have more than one sexual partner at certain periods.
Thus decontextualized, the customs became incomprehensible and
were viewed as "primitive" (Ahlberg, 1991).

In the wake of various social and political upheavals, traditional
social regulations and control systems have broken down. The
cultural meaning of sexual relationships is widely confused. According

to Ahlberg (1993), one can isolate four types of moral regime including the Christian, the "traditional" African, administrative/legal and the more secular romantic love. They mainly advocate sexual abstinence, although secular agencies have a less aggressive approach, instead emphasizing "safer sex". But the adult regimes operate in a vacuum since they do not have the mechanisms to regulate and control the young. The teenagers, therefore, face a paradoxical situation of prohibition, silence and confusion from the adult world. Contrary to what happened in the past, the public discourse on sexuality is largely silenced and relationships are hidden (Ahlberg, 1993).

However, it is commonly believed that regular sexual intercourse maintains the health and sanity of both men and women. Both genders are believed to have strong sexual drives, which must find regular release (Udvardy, 1988).

Mbilinyi (1985) raises the issue of female sexuality and fertility with regard to social behaviour and state control. She notes that there was a growing concern in Tanzania about the "bad behaviour" of the youth and especially of "young girls", and challenges the concept of "bad". In popular discourse, bad behaviour includes

school pregnancies, induced abortions and baby-dumping, sexual promiscuity and prostitution, rural-urban migration of young women, rudeness and lewd language and the disobedience of girls when faced with paternal demands for marriage. (Mbilinyi, 1985:111)

It should be noted here that all the forms of bad behaviour listed are those which affect girls, and nothing is said about the bad behaviour of boys.

Mbilinyi also observed factors which influence teenage behaviour, such as life in town, where sometimes a whole family is forced to sleep in one room. Another factor is lack of communication between parents and children because parents have no time to attend to children due to the pressures of work for economic survival. At the same time, she considered the possibility that these forms of behaviour could be signs of protest against control in favour of social change.

The most far-reaching sanction on female sexuality is the government rule for expelling pregnant school girls. Families, however, expect that girls will engage in sex only after marriage. Early marriages were common in most communities as a means of forestalling premarital sex and pregnancy (Kassimoto, 1987). These expectations become more difficult to achieve because of the widening gap between physical maturity and the socially accepted marriageable age. A number of factors contribute to this gap, including completion of one's education and a girl's desire to engage in economic activities before marrying. I, therefore, found it important to explore the forms of resistance and conformity that girls used in dealing with the control of their sexuality and how they managed to handle the different pressures which confronted them in their communities.

Most of the unmarried teenage mothers I interviewed regarded heterosexual intercourse as normal and natural. More than half of the teenage mothers wondered how one could evade sexual intercourse. Their main questions were:
– For how long should one postpone sex?
– What is the right age to start having sex?

Some of them said that they were terrified of having sexual intercourse before they finished school. After finishing school, most of the unmarried mothers said that they saw no reason why they should wait any longer. However, a third of them said they waited for a while before they started to engage in sexual intercourse.

All these teenage mothers admitted learning about sex through discussions with peers. Parents and relatives were not willing to tell them openly what they needed to know.

All the married girls were unwilling to talk about their sexual experiences because they had been taught during the bride's send-off ceremony that the coital experience of a married woman is a secret of the couple: *ngono ni kunga za unyumba*. Moreover, most of them believed that conception was God's will and that it was a blessing. One girl even considered it a miracle and was convinced that there was no way that one could stop it from happening if it were God's wish.

Teenage mothers' age at menarche

The menarche age for the mothers studied ranges between ten and sixteen years. While an equal number of the seniors had their menarche at thirteen and fourteen years, the majority of the juniors had their menarche at thirteen years of age and only three had it at fourteen years (see Table 17). The preceding figures show that the age at menarche is apparently decreasing.

Table 17. *Menarche age of teenage mothers by group*

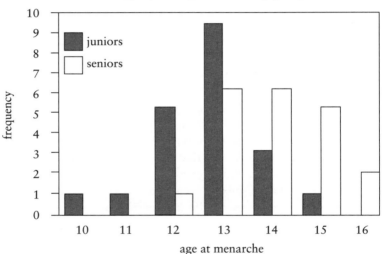

age at menarche

The decrease in age at menarche is not peculiar to this group. Statistics from Kenya show that the average age at menarche has continued to fall. In a study done in the late 1970s, it was shown that while the menarche-age average for women over nineteen years was 14.4 years, that of college girls was 12.9 years (Gyepi-Garbrah, 1985). In Nigeria, the average age at menarche has continued to fall from 14 years in the early 1960s to 13.85 in late 1960s and 12.3 in recent years (Gyepi-Garbrah, 1985b).

All these studies, however, do not take the nutritional status of the interviewees into consideration. This status has been proved to be one of the major factors in decreasing the age at menarche and increasing fertility (Gyepi-Garbrah, 1985).

What teenage mothers know about menarche and conception

I found that most of the girls learned about menarche when they had it, i.e., their mothers or other female relatives explained it to them only after seeing their first menstrual blood. When asked about their understanding of menarche at the time they had it, about one-third of the teenage mothers, mainly from the junior group, admitted that though they had heard the term *kuvunja ungo* (menarche in Kiswahili), which literally means "breaking the winnowing basket", they did not know what to expect. They knew the term but had no understanding of the concept. Nevertheless, they all said that they knew that it had nothing to do with its literal meaning.

Almost all of them said that they were frightened at the sight of blood. One of them from Ujiji, who had her menarche at the age of ten, said she even went into hiding, thinking that she had contracted bilharzia by swimming in the lake, something she had been warned against many times by her mother. Even when her mother learned that the girl had seen the blood, she could not believe that it was menstrual blood. It was only when she had her period for the third time that the mother told her that *amekua* (she had matured).

Table 18. *Information on menarche by age*

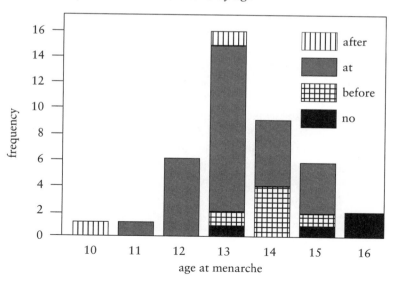

Another one-third of the teenage mothers said that they understood menarche as one of the signs of maturity in a girl. They admitted that though they did not know exactly what to expect on the day that watavunja ungo (when they will have menarche), they knew that on that day they would reach what they called *usichana* (girlhood), and they were looking forward to it. Other signs of "girlhood" mentioned (and appreciated) were the growing of breasts and the shaping of the body. As Mwanaisha put it, *"nilipoanza kuota maziwa, dada zangu waliniambia kuwa karibu nitavunja ungo na ndio usichana huo"* (when the breasts started to grow, my sisters told me that I will soon have my menarche, and that is girlhood).

The stage before girlhood was identified by most of them as *utoto* (childhood), which did not seem to be as appealing as girlhood.

Therefore, to most of these girls, menarche is an important stage of growing up and is accepted with pride; that now they are "girls" and they have left their childhood behind them.

Among the forty girls that participated in the study, only six had learned beforehand what menarche was. One of the girls from Dar es Salaam was told by her grandmother, while the other was taught at a before-advent-of-menarche initiation ceremony. For the Ujiji teenage mothers, two got the information from peers at school, and the other two (both from the senior group) were told by or had seen their sisters when they had gone through it. As opposed to many of the teenage mothers above, the six knew that the sight of menstrual blood for the first time was a sign of menarche, but what some of them did not know was that bleeding was going to be a monthly affair.

There are indications that age is a factor in a girl's urge to seek information about menarche and related phenomena. In both Dar es Salaam and Ujiji, among the girls who sought and got information on menarche before they had it, most of them had their menarche at fourteen years (see Table 18). All those who had their menarche before thirteen learned about it either at menarche or after.

Table 19. *Source of information on menarche and relationship between menarche and conception*

Source	juniors		seniors	
type	1	2	1	2
mother	9	6	7	6
relative	6	5	9	6
peers	3	5	0	5
maid	1	0	0	0
ceremony	0	0	1	1
classes	0	2	0	3
no information	1	3	3	0
Total	20	*	20	*

Notes: type 1 - information on menarche

      2 - information on menarche/conception

     * - some received information from more than one source

The major source of information on menarche in the junior group is the mother, who was the source of information for nine of them. In the senior group, relatives (especially grandmothers and maternal aunts) were more frequently the source of information, although closely followed by the mother (see Table 19). This mirrors changing conditions, because in the past, the role of imparting knowledge about sexuality and conception was played by persons other than the parents. Commonly, relationships between generations next to each other were restricted and excluded discussions about sexual matters, while the relations between alternate generations, i.e., between grandparents and grandchildren, were close, easy and involved intimate issues. The grandmothers often initiated the girls into the mysteries of sexuality and fertility (Vuyk, 1991).

However, quite a number of teenage mothers from both the junior and the senior groups had experienced their menarche but had not been told by anyone that they had done so until they fell pregnant: one from the junior group (who had her menarche at thirteen and fell pregnant a few months later) and three from the senior group who had their menarche at fifteen and sixteen years.

None of the teenage mothers really abhorred menstruation, but some of them found its monthly repetition onerous. As Kostash (1989:229) observes in her study of Canadian teenage girls, none of the teenage mothers interviewed said that she disliked being a young woman. As far as the relationship between menstruation and reproductive capability is concerned, one-third of the girls were told by the same relatives who had informed them on menarche that they could fall pregnant after having their first menstruation. Some of the girls learned this from peers, usually after menarche. Some were also informed by relatives, while a few had peers as their sole source of knowledge regarding the relationship between menarche and conception.

There are also a number of girls who learned about the relationship between menarche and fertility from science or domestic science classes at school, especially after the fifth year of primary education, when most of them had already had their menarche. One girl had read about it in a book she had bought. There were also three junior girls who knew that they had already had their menarche but were not informed about their capability to conceive until after they fell pregnant.

Only one girl from Dar es Salaam admitted that she was taught about the "safe period" by her mother at menarche. Nonetheless, it seems that the information she got was incorrect. She was told that it is not safe to have sex just before or soon after having her period, i.e., the in-between time was the safe period. Consequently, she fell pregnant a few months after menarche.

It is evident, therefore, that the girls learn about conception too late to be able to take any precautions. "In many instances, girls get pregnant out of sheer ignorance of the consequences of involving themselves in sexual activities"(Kassimoto, 1987). If a girl has to wait for this knowledge until menarche, one of the most important signs of reproductive capability, then it could be too late.

Knowledge of labour and childbirth

Most of the girls learned of the signs of labour only through immediate experience. In this sample of forty teenage mothers, for example, about half of them were told about labour as it occurred and most of them could only define the process according to their own experiences. Many of them gave answers like, "I cannot explain the term because I did not experience the process". Such an answer was given by half the teenage mothers in explaining *kuvunja* chupa (rupture of membranes) which is apparently an important stage of labour (see also discussion below on Giving birth, and *tumbo la zingizi*, afterpains).

Both the girls and the midwives admitted that the girls faced childbirth without adequate knowledge of child-bearing and post-partum care.

I talked to sixteen midwives, twelve of them were nurses/midwives and four were traditional midwives. To obtain interviewees who were conventional midwives, the formal administrative channels of the hospital and clinic were used. I divided the conventional health aides into two groups with equal numbers from each group: those who had worked as midwives for more than four years, termed senior midwives, and those who had worked for less than that time, whom I called junior midwives.

I selected the traditional midwives at Ujiji through an old acquaintance who is herself a traditional midwife. She knew the other midwives as they met regularly and shared information on their trade. The traditional midwives came exclusively from Ujiji, as I could not find any in Dar es Salaam.

Traditional midwives' services to teenage mothers

The four traditional midwives, whose ages ranged from fifty to seventy years, stated that they no longer practise their skills as frequently as before because mothers deliver in hospitals. They usually only attend those who fail to get transport to the hospital. Most of the deliveries they conduct are normal. They refer the complicated cases to hospitals as soon as they suspect that there is going to be a difficult delivery.

They do, however, render other services, such as turning the foetus when they anticipate a breech delivery and sometimes they give herbs to mothers to help them deliver safely, especially when the labour goes on for too long. Two of them said they are sometimes called, usually by mothers of the expectant teenage mothers, to instruct the girls on labour management, usually from the sixth month of pregnancy, because some might deliver prematurely.

When it came to the use of terms and their meanings, they said that they normally instruct the girls in the same language that they use during delivery and show them the different positions that can be used during childbirth. They also teach the girls how to push, and they tell them that they will feel like they want to pass stool when they are about to deliver. Other terms that the traditional midwives felt necessary to inform the girls of concern the rupture of membranes, which they held to be an important aspect of labour.

When I asked them about the *waters*, all the traditional midwives described them as green in colour. This colour was also mentioned by the girls who had received instructions from the traditional midwives, thus showing that the girls could at least repeat the instructions. However, the conventional midwives I interviewed in Kigoma said that green waters depict fetal distress (see also Myles, 1975).

Another term that the traditional midwives were interested in commenting upon is *kondo la nyuma* (afterbirth). In Kigoma the most commonly used variant of the term is bebeo (baby carrier). It is believed by all the interviewed traditional midwives that delay in expulsion of the afterbirth is detrimental to the baby. At first, I was puzzled by this belief, but after consulting conventional midwives at the regional hospital in Kigoma, I was informed that the expulsion of the afterbirth activates the fall of oestriol and allows prolactin to initiate lactation (see also Myles, 1975). Normally, mothers are encouraged to breast-feed as soon as they can, usually within one hour of delivery.

Deliveries by traditional midwives are usually done with the help of at least two of the girl's relatives, one to help hold the girl and the other to pass the equipment, e.g., razor, thread, clothes, and to boil water. There is always someone with the girl, who is never left alone.

As Anderson and Staugård (1986) observed of deliveries by

traditional midwives in Botswana, the delivering mother, can, with the help of relatives, choose a position that is comfortable for delivery and other members of the family keep close watch until delivery is completed. Most of the midwives said there is some rejoicing, especially by ululation, to mark a safe delivery.

How do conventional midwives relate to teenage mothers?

Services for mothers are divided into antenatal care and delivery care. In my study I felt it made sense to separate antenatal care from delivery care; hence the mother is faced by two groups of nurses/ midwives; those who examine her at the antenatal clinic and those who attend to her during delivery at the labour ward and after. The only information that the labour ward nurse has about the patient is her antenatal card. As for the delivering mother, usually she has never seen the midwife before delivery.

What is learned at an antenatal clinic? I visited three such clinics: two in Dar es Salaam at a referral and a district hospital respectively, and one in Kigoma town since there was no clinic operating in Ujiji. All the clinics were operated under the Maternal and Child Health programme (MCH).

MCH clinics were started so as to offer comprehensive services to mother and child. The services include immunization; nutrition surveillance; prenatal and postnatal care; assistance during labour and delivery; education on the above; family planning; malaria chemoprophylaxis and treatment of minor health problems (Ministry of Health, 1982).

All the antenatal clinics visited offered the mother-to-be some instruction before physical examinations began. However, it was noted that most of the expectant mothers came after instruction time. Hence, thirteen teenage mothers in the sample said that they had received no instruction at the antenatal clinics (see Table 20).

The most common topics of instruction are nutrition and cleanliness, cited by about half the teenage mothers. Other frequently cited subjects, in order of citation by teenage mothers, were preparation of the baby's articles (clothes, soap, etc.), importance of immunization and family planning (FP). Only one teenage mother reported that she had received some instruction on the stages of labour and labour management during a tête-à-tête with a friendly nurse.

Table 20. *Instruction at the antenatal clinic as cited by teenage mothers*

Subject	cat.	no.	nutri-tion	clean-liness	baby article	immuni-zation	FP	other*
Dar es Salaam	1	3	3	4	2	2	0	0
	2	0	4	1	5	1	1	0
Ujiji	1	2	3	3	1	3	2	4
	2	8	1	2	1	0	1	0
Total**		13	11	10	9	6	4	4

Notes: cat. 1 – Junior teenage mothers
       2 – Senior teenage mothers
      * – include exercising and resting
     ** – some cited more than one subject

However, most of the girls appeared unsatisfied with the methods of instruction. They were usually general lectures given to a mixed audience of girls and adults. The girls did not feel comfortable in the presence of the adult women, as they considered these adult women as being comparable to their mothers. Furthermore, the girls reported that the subjects were repeated so often that they lost interest. Hence, the most important thing to them was the physical examination and the medicines that they received at the clinic.

Giving birth

About half the teenage mothers said that they learned about labour as it occurred. Most of the girls who had learned about childbirth prior to delivery were informed by peers who had already delivered. Therefore, most of the girls in labour did not know when the critical moment had been reached and when they should call the midwife. According to the girls, what scared them most was the fact that they could have given birth without any help. Some of them reported that they mainly relied on adult mothers to guide them on when to call for the midwife, or the adults themselves called the midwives for the girls.

Apparently, most of the girls felt that there was too much of a patient–nurse relationship in hospital deliveries, i.e., they felt as though they were sick when they went for delivery at the hospital.

Another problem that the teenage mothers reported was lack of communication during childbirth, especially on labour management. Personal experience of childbirth seemed to be one of the main factors affecting the ability to communicate effectively with primigravidae and especially with those who were under age and needed a lot of attention and support.

The problem seemed more acute for the junior midwives. In the course of the interviews, it became apparent that Asha, a midwife who had not experienced childbirth herself, could not adequately explain to primigravidae how to manage labour. For example, in defining *push*, she could neither offer an equivalent nor elaborate, while those who had given birth likened it to *kujikema/kunya mavi magumu*, passing a hard stool. This was also the definition given by the majority of the teenage mothers.

When asked about the terms that they used at the labour ward, all the midwives seemed to be more comfortable with English terms and used Kiswahili terms only when they were talking directly to a delivering mother. For example, all the conventional midwives said that they preferred to use *placenta* and uterus even if the whole conversation was in Kiswahili, rather than *kondo la nyuma or mji wa mimba* respectively. The most frequent Kiswahili terms used in communication with delivering mothers are *kuvunja chupa* (rupture of membranes), which literally translates as "breaking the bottle" and *kusukuma* (to push). One of the key questions a woman in labour is asked is whether she has already ruptured the membranes.

Some of the midwives admitted that the term *kuvunja chupa* is sometimes not understood by primigravidae, especially those who are very young, as they confuse it with its literal meaning. In such cases, the midwives ask the girl if she has had any discharge from the genitals. Then the girl might speak about a slippery discharge with traces of blood which is commonly known as the "show" or she

Teenage mothers need more instruction about sexuality and reproductive health than what is offered now; it is too little and comes too late.
Photo: Charlotte Thege, Bazaar Bildbyrå, Stockholm

might talk about a release of the "waters".

Another term which is commonly used in the labour ward is *placenta*. The word *placenta* will usually be used even in Kiswahili conversations among the midwives. When asked in which context they use the term, all the midwives said that it is usually when there is a delay in the expulsion of the placenta or some trouble with it, otherwise they do not use it.

Another variant to the term *kondo la nyuma* (placenta) is *salio* which was mentioned to the researcher by one senior midwife in Dar es Salaam who has worked in a number of villages around the city, where the term is more commonly used than *kondo la nyuma* (the district hospital visited in Dar es Salaam serves mothers from the villages). It was only this single senior midwife who knew the term *salio* in Dar es Salaam, and none of the other midwives interviewed in the area knew the variant. On the other hand, all the midwives interviewed in Kigoma knew the frequently used term in the community, *bebeo*, but admitted that they rarely used it.

Also, the teenage mothers said that the nurses ordered them to do things without explaining why. Most of them stated that they were ordered to sleep on their sides without being told why they had to do so. As Myles puts it:

It is essential for the peace of most women (and the teenage mothers are no exceptions), that they be kept informed regarding the progress they are making. Women respond magnificently to a word of praise, and being given reasons or explanations... Women who scream during labour do so more from fear than pain, and the midwife should communicate confidence by her calm, competent bearing and kind actions. (Myles, 1975:228)

It seems that many conventional midwives forget this very important aspect of midwifery, i.e., putting the mother at ease. The midwives normally concentrate on the job of delivering the baby and performing their routine tasks. This could be a result of overwork, as most of the midwives complained of understaffing, especially in labour wards and, more crucially, during the night shift.

Too little too late

It is evident from the study that teenage mothers need more information on sexuality and reproductive health than what is now offered in the society: this is too little and comes too late. As has been shown by the study, most of the girls learned about menstruation and the capability to conceive at menarhce or after. The first ovulation takes place before menarche. Hence it is possible for a girl to fall pregnant without having her menarche. Furthermore, though mothers and other female relatives are willing to tell the girl about menarche, conception and procreation, i.e., warning the girl about conception, they do not elaborate on the whole reproductive process. Consequently, teenage girls often find themselves confused by the misinformation that they gather from unreliable sources of knowledge such as peers.

Furthermore, the study shows that mothers have been the major source of information, especially for junior teenage mothers, i.e., those who have their first childbirths between fourteen and seventeen years of age. Yet the mothers are themselves not properly informed about the reproductive process. Also, some beliefs and misinformation might have an adverse effect on family planning programmes. For example, there are the beliefs that conception is a miracle and that the "safe days" are those which are in between the periods, rather than at the beginning and end of the cycle.

Teenage mothers also indicated a need for more communication between themselves and the midwives. They need information on labour ward care and procedures, and on how to manage labour and childbirth. There are indications that conventional midwives talk about teenage mothers among themselves in terms that the teenage mothers do not understand, thus creating uncertainty. This type of discourse is the opposite of the desired norm, i.e., talking to the teenage mothers and assuring them about the whole process.

However, I found that senior midwives were better than junior midwives at dealing with teenage mothers and could use explanatory terms that the teenage mothers understood. The senior midwives seemed to be able to communicate better and were acquainted with the language of the communities which they served.

As for the traditional midwives, there are indications that the trade is dying out due to the fact that many deliveries take place in hospitals and that traditional deliveries only happen when the mother cannot make it to hospital. Most of the traditional midwives admitted that they do not offer as much assistance during delivery due to the fact that hospitals have better and safer services and can deal much better with complications.

Also, though they have valid knowledge, for example that delayed expulsion of placenta will harm the well-being of the baby, they usually do not have an explanation for such phenomena. Hence, this knowledge is often discredited as it lacks scientific explanation. One conventional midwife even dismissed the ability of traditional midwives to turn breech babies. She remarked:

Normally babies turn on their own when they are ready for delivery. If it was true that the traditional midwives were able to turn the foetus to a vertex position, there would not have been breech deliveries in communities that have traditional midwives.

However, the belief is well established that traditional midwives do turn would-be breech babies to a vertex position, and many mothers who anticipate breech deliveries do go for such service and do then deliver normally.

In addition, I also learned that some mothers take their teenage pregnant girls to traditional midwives for instruction on labour and childbirth. Such instruction seemed to help the teenage mothers cope well with labour and childbirth. All the teenage mothers who had received such instruction showed a better understanding of reproductive health and seemed to be more at ease during the interview than their counterparts who had not received such instruction. Such instruction is not offered by conventional health facilities. Moreover, the instruction that is offered by conventional health facilities is given in mixed groups, i.e., people of all ages, and repeated so many times that listeners lose interest. Most of the teenage mothers did not feel comfortable about receiving instruction on reproductive health and family planning in a mixed group of adults and girls.

Also, senior midwives, and especially those who have already gone through the child-bearing experience, should be assigned to work in the special clinics and in the labour wards that deal with teenage mothers.

It is essential to develop a more holistic approach to childbirth in hospital settings, so that the mother feels that she is experiencing a natural phenomenon. Furthermore, cultural issues of the communities have to be taken into consideration, as long as they do not interfere with the child-bearing process and the health of the mother and the newly born baby. It is also important that conventional midwives familiarize themselves with the languages and terminologies used by the communities they work with and use them as much as possible when they are in the company of the local people.

The above comments indicate how reproduction has been narrowed down to a medical and technical issue. The process of "medicalization" has stemmed from transformations within Western medicine – and it has meant that the procreation of life has ceased to be part of the moral and social order.

On the other hand, there is a need to impart more scientific knowledge on childbirth to traditional midwives so that they can offer safer services.

References

Ahlberg, Beth Maina, 1991, *Women, Sexuality and the Changing Social Order.* Philadelphia: Gordon and Breach Science Publishers S.A.

Ahlberg, Beth Maina, 1993, "Is there a Distinct African Sexuality?" Dept. of International Health Care Research (IHCAR), Karolinska Institute, Stockholm, and Department of Sociology, Uppsala University.

Anderson, S., and F. Staugård, 1986, *Traditional midwives.* Gaberone: Ipelegeng Publishers.

Gyepi-Garbrah, B., 1985, *Adolescent fertility in Kenya.* Watertown, Massachusetts: The Pathfinder Fund.

Gyepi-Garbrah, B., 1985b, *Adolescent fertility in Nigeria.* Watertown, Massachusetts: The Pathfinder Fund.

Kaisi, M., 1976, *Ukunga na utunzaji wa watoto vijijini (Midwifery and child care in rural areas).* Dar es Salaam: Tanzania Publishing House.

Kassimoto, T.J., 1985, *Attitudes of Parents, Students, Ex-Pregnant School Girls and Administrators on the Expulsion of Pregnant Girls from Schools: A Case Study of Dar es Salaam and Mbeya Regions.* Unpublished M.A. Dissertation, University of Dar es Salaam.

Kostash, M., 1989, No Kidding: *Inside the world of teenage girls.* Toronto: McClelland and Stewart.

Mbilinyi, M.J., 1984, "Research priorities in women's studies in Eastern Africa", *Women's Studies International Forum*, 7, 4, 289–300.

Mbilinyi, M.J., 1985, "Struggles concerning sexuality among female youth", *Journal of Eastern African Research and Development* 15, 111–123. Nairobi: Gideon S. Were Press.

Ministry of Health, United Republic of Tanzania, 1982, *Evaluation of the MCH Programme.* Dar es Salaam: Ministry of Health.

Myles, M.F., 1971, *A textbook for midwives with modern concepts of obstetrics and neonatal care, 7th edition.* London: Longman Group Ltd.

Myles, M.F., 1975, *A textbook for midwives with modern concepts of obstetrics and neonatal care, 8th edition.* London: Longman Group Ltd.

Phoenix, Ann, 1991, *Young Mothers?* Cambridge: Polity Press.

Polomé, E. 1967, *Swahili language handbook*. Washington D.C.: Centre for Applied Linguistics.

Tippu, Tip, 1966, *Maisha ya Hamed bin Muhammed el Murjebi.* Nairobi: East African Literature Bureau.

Udvardy, Monica, 1988, *Social and cultural dimensions for research on sexual behaviour*, Society and HIV/AIDS, Karolinska Institute, Department of International Health Care Research.

Vuyk, T., 1991, *Children of one Womb. Leiden:* Centre of Non-Western Studies.

9. Adolescent mothers

Alice Rugumyamheto, Virginia Kainamula and
Juliana Mziray

We decided to undertake this study because we felt there was a need
to find out how much teenagers know about reproduction, what
they think and feel about becoming mothers and how they cope with
life during pregnancy and the period of child rearing. We also
wanted to find out how much they know about family planning
methods.

During this study, we traced the life of the pregnant teenagers
from mid-pregnancy (five to six months) until after delivery. Our
study was conducted in the Morogoro and Dar es Salaam regions.
In Morogoro, we visited Kilosa and Morogoro townships, while in
Dar es Salaam, we visited Ilala, Kinondoni and Temeke districts.

A total of 120 expectant teenage girls between thirteen and
eighteen years of age were interviewed. One-third of them lived in
rural areas, while the rest lived in the urban areas. The expectant
teenagers were identified (with the assistance of a nurse) and semi-
structured interviews were undertaken at the Maternal and Child
Health Centres (MCH).

Three months after their delivery, we visited and talked to fifteen
teenage mothers and their parents. In addition, we also interviewed
some doctors, nurses and social welfare workers.

We used both structured and unstructured questions. The first
interview was carried out during pregnancy, and the second after
delivery.

When we asked the girls about their marital status, many of
them (about 52 per cent) said that they were not married. On
average, the majority were in the fifteen to sixteen year age-group.
We were amazed to find that ten of our respondents were in the
thirteen to fourteen year age-group.

We wanted to learn from the expectant teenagers whether this
was their first pregnancy and the number of live children they had.
In response, the majority indicated that the pregnancy was their first

one, and a few of them said that it was their second, while two reported that their first borns had died.

Many of the girls informed us that they came from low-income families where the main source of income was subsistence farming and petty business. In Tanzania, families which depend on such activities can hardly cope with the cost of living. Because of their socio-economic conditions, most of the parents become very disappointed when they learn that their daughters are pregnant. Obviously, this means an extra burden financially, since the teenage girls have no means to support themselves.

Knowledge about reproductive health

When we asked the girls about their knowledge of reproductive matters, we learned that although half of them knew that pregnancy occurs after engagement in sexual intercourse, they were not able to point out the exact period in a woman's monthly cycle when pregnancy occurs. We also found that half the girls were ignorant of the unsafe and safe periods.

We learned that adolescent girls are sometimes partially informed and sometimes misinformed about pregnancy. For instance, when some of the girls missed their monthly periods they wrongly associated this with something else, e.g., changes in the weather, medication etc. *Halima*, for example, who was sixteen years old, told us that she had moved from a cold climate up-country to Dar es Salaam, which is hot. When she missed her periods she thought this was due to the change in climate. Another girl had developed frequent malaria attacks and was given strong medication by a doctor. When she missed her periods, she thought this was a side-effect of the malaria drugs. On further questioning, she admitted having had a sexual relationship and told us she never expected to conceive while taking malaria tablets.

For example, a thirteen year old girl had the following experience of menarche:

I had my menarche when I was twelve. Before I got initiated I had an affair with a boyfriend and never got my menstruation again. I noticed that my breasts were growing bigger and the school uniform becoming tighter, but thought I had put on weight. When I was taken to the hospital they found out that I was five months pregnant. Since I had had a sexual relationship with a schoolboy only once, I did not expect that I would conceive.

Another girl of sixteen years told us:

I had irregular periods so I visited a doctor who gave me tetracycline capsules. After the treatment, my periods stopped but I was not worried because my friends had earlier informed me that tetracycline tablets can be used as contraceptive pills.

On further questioning, this girl informed us that her friends use aspirin tablets and local herbs as contraceptives.

The experiences of these four girls bear witness to the ignorance of our adolescent girls about contraception and reproductive issues in general.

Preparations for delivery and childcare

Balanced diet, clean and loose clothes, physical exercise and a suitable sleeping place were mentioned by the expectant teenagers as the basic requirements for a pregnant woman. The girls were also aware that there is a need to attend antenatal clinics regularly. This information was obtained either from parents, friends, neighbours or even from magazines and radio programmes. Although all the girls had learned from the above sources that they needed to prepare items for the unborn baby, a few indicated that they had not prepared anything. Because of the beliefs of their respective ethnic groups, it was taboo to prepare anything before the baby was born, especially clothes, the girls told us. Buying clothes before the child is born can be a bad omen. For those who did buy some items prior to delivery, the most common were clothes, washing basins, and baby cots.

More than half the girls stated that they had received some instruction regarding the indications of labour from their mothers or from relatives with whom they were staying. Discharge of water or blood, often associated with several types of stomach-ache, was interpreted as the only sign of labour. *Anna*, a sixteen year old pregnant girl, disagreed with this information and related her elder sister's experience. "My sister was taken unawares by severe vomiting. When she reached the hospital, the doctor who examined her confirmed that she was in labour. Half an hour later she delivered a baby boy".

"I suspect there are other signs of labour", another girl remarked. "My sister Mtawo told me that not all the women in the labour ward complained of stomach-ache." Asked about other complaints, she said: "She told me some women complained of headaches and backache; others just walked to and from the toilet without a specific complaint." Those who were not taught the indications of labour said they hoped a definite change would occur, then they would inform an elderly person who had experienced childbirth.

Regarding childcare, all the girls agreed that a newly born baby needs special care. Only half of them claimed to be knowledgeable about caring for a young baby. They had gained this knowledge while taking care of their younger sisters and brothers. The rest feared that caring for younger sisters and brothers or even living with women who had young children provided them with knowledge that was too limited. "I only know that a young baby is washed differently from older ones, and that the mother would breast-feed it", said *Amina*, a seventeen year old expectant girl. "With that small amount of information, I am not confident enough to take on the difficult task of child-rearing", she added.

"Baby care is not an easy thing. I expect to be guided by my mother as I go on doing it", another girl said. Several girls mentioned that they had listened to some radio programmes and others had read magazines that contained some information on childcare, but complained that these were either too academic or written in English, which they could not understand well.

Reactions of the girls' parents, relatives and neighbours

The reactions of the expectant girls differed when they first realized
that they were pregnant. To almost all the married ones, this was
good news and regarded as a success. In many societies, a woman is
expected to fall pregnant soon after marriage. A delay causes
suspicion that the woman is not fertile and can endanger the stability
of the marriage. However, for *Anna*, it was different. She was
married at the age of fifteen and was afraid of pregnancy
complications. "I did not expect it so soon, I am still too young", she
complained.

To unmarried girls, especially the ones who were still in school,
who were rejected by their boy-friends, the news about being
pregnant was a source of misery. Many of them showed distress
about being pregnant. "What have I done?", *Emmy* asked in
desperation. "Where shall I go?", another girl wondered. "What
will I tell my parents?", a confused *Hawa* cried. "Who will help me
in this disaster?", *Emmy* kept on asking herself. According to several
girls, this was the beginning of hard times for them.

A common worry among the girls was the reaction of their
parents because they all knew that pregnancy out of wedlock is
unacceptable to many societies in the area. *Ramatu*, a fifteen year
old Standard 7 student, encountered and experienced bitterness.
Her story was that her parents had thrown her out of their home
after a letter arrived from her schoolmaster stating that a medical
examination had revealed that she was pregnant. Ramatu went to
her aunt who was unwilling to accept her. She tried her uncle who
also rejected her. The parents were furious because she could no
longer continue at school, thereby denying herself higher education
and the possibility of good employment. Usually, parents have high
expectations that their children will get a good education which will
enable them to get a good job and thus be able to help the parents
financially. Neighbours advised her to seek help from a local social
welfare officer who offered rehabilitation services. Efforts by the
social welfare officer, who visited Ramatu's parents, were rewarded
after two weeks when she was accepted back home. No action was
taken against Ramatu's boy-friend. He continued with his studies.
Such painful incidents are common in these areas. According to this

particular social welfare officer, his office had offered rehabilitation services to several pregnant girls that year.

Unmarried expectant girls face problems with neighbours also. *Faya*, a sixteen year old ex-primary school leaver was impregnated by a secondary school student. Neighbours despised her and insulted her. No girls were allowed to talk to her, lest she teach them bad ways. "The thing I hated most was being suspected of having had sexual activities with any man on the road", *Faya* claimed. "When no man accepts paternity, you are suspected of having affairs with anyone, even if you have never talked to them."

Because most of the girls came from families who made their living by farming and from petty business, they had financial problems as they could not count on a reliable income. One girl mentioned that pregnancy would delay her chances of getting married in the near future because she needed time to take care of the baby. "My chances of getting married to a decent man are very slight." "In my community no decent man would be attracted to a girl who has had a child out of wedlock", another girl lamented. All these examples show the girls' negative attitudes towards pregnancy out of wedlock.

Blaming the mothers

A teenager's pregnancy is always kept secret. The first person to be informed about it is carefully selected. About one-third of the teenagers first informed their mothers; another one-third informed their boy-friends or husbands. The remaining turned to trusted close relatives or friends.

Mothers showed dissatisfaction with their daughters' premature and premarital pregnancies. We asked the mothers to describe the problems which they had encountered after their daughters became pregnant:

–She is always sick; dehydrated and weak
– Early pregnancies make us suffer because we have to provide financial support and care to both the mother and the child
– My daughter did not admit to the pregnancy for *six* months, so when I realized she was pregnant I immediately took her to the clinic for a check-up

– My daughter was fourteen when she conceived. After delivery she could not take care of herself, or the baby, so I had to do everything for her and wake her up at night to breast-feed the baby
– When she got pregnant she deceived us by saying that she was sick. We wasted a lot of time taking her to the hospital since she was anaemic. Later we discovered that she was sick due to pregnancy and we got really mad.

When we asked the mothers to express the feelings of their husbands upon learning about the pregnancy of the daughters, some of the reactions expressed were:
– He was very disappointed but tried to bear it
– He was angry and blamed me for not taking care of our daughter
– He lamented that the pregnancy had brought shame to him
– He said that I had conspired with our daughter to perform evil deeds
– He accepted it, knowing that nowadays it is normal for teenagers to become pregnant.

The community blamed the parents for not counselling their daughters. Others blamed the girls for disobeying the parents and members of the community. A few people in the community were sympathetic to the pregnant teenagers. The majority had mixed feelings towards teenage pregnancy.

Very few parents admitted that their daughters had attended ritual ceremonies such as *unyago* and *mkoleni* (sex education). They claimed that religion forbids such activities and the practices are regarded as primitive. Those who practice *unyago* said that it is performed when the daughter reaches puberty, i.e., at thirteen to fourteen years. Some of the things they learn during *unyago* include:
– healthcare of the body, particularly during menstruation
– how to live with a husband
– symptoms of pregnancy
– how to be discreet, particularly regarding female affairs
– how to respect traditional customs
– respect for adults.

All the parents interviewed admitted that they *had not* taught their daughters about the biological changes which take place during puberty. Most of them claimed that by tradition it was improper for them to educate their children, because normally this was done by an elderly person, such as a grandmother or aunt of the adolescent.

The aftermath of delivery

A majority of the expectant mothers delivered in hospitals and three-quarters of them had safe deliveries. A few delivered at home and only one girl delivered on her way to hospital. The complicated cases we came across were Caesarean sections. One teenage girl died after such an operation. Prolonged deliveries, eclampsia, and cases of anaemia were traced from hospital records. One teenage mother was still in hospital four months after delivery because she had suffered a serious back injury. She could not move her limbs. Another fourteen year old mother remained in hospital for several months because she ruptured her bladder during delivery. Two girls had stillbirths. At the completion of the study, three more girls had died; one of AIDS, another of tuberculosis, and the third of anaemia.

The teenagers who delivered for the first time had a number of comments on labour pains. "The pains were very severe", said *Cecilia*, a seventeen year old mother. "I wonder how some women manage to give birth to as many as ten children."

Susanna said she could not contemplate another delivery. One girl who had a stillbirth explained that the pains had disturbed her mentally and that she had no control of herself. She thought that this was the reason her child had died. "I do not believe other women suffered as much pain as I did", she added. Several teenage mothers said that the labour pains were severe enough to kill a woman and definitely shorten one's life.

Although most of the teenage mothers who delivered in hospitals praised the nurses and doctors as helpful and loving, they complained about the presence of older women in the labour ward. One girl remembered one elderly woman mocking her by saying: "You thought it was ice-cream. Taste the sweetness of it now." "They had no sympathy for me", another girl complained. "They laughed loudly when I was crying for help", she recalled. "You hurried for it. Don't disturb us", they shouted and kept on laughing.

Nurses and doctors at the hospitals do face problems when

attending expectant teenagers during delivery. "Some girls are very uncooperative when you give them useful instructions", a nurse informed us. "Some refuse to undress and to allow their genital parts to be examined, especially by male medical staff." One nurse cited the example of a girl who refused to follow instructions and instead decided to fight the nurse. Nurses frequently have to ask for the watchman's assistance in catching teenage girls who run away from the labour ward. Such behaviour may necessitate a Caesarean operation.

Several cases were a cause of surprise to the attending doctors and nurses. One doctor mentioned that he once encountered a pregnant girl who was a virgin (hymen intact). He tried to explore the girl's life, but could not get much information because the girl kept on crying. She was too young, the doctor remembered. "I could not understand how she fell pregnant." Another doctor came across a girl who reached puberty at the age of eleven and was pregnant at twelve. "There was no way out, she had to deliver by operation", the doctor insisted. "Such cases are becoming common nowadays."

Being a mother

"How did you feel when you first saw your baby?", we asked the new mothers. They responded by saying:
– Happier than ever before in my life
– Victorious. I have proved to the world that I am a woman
– I cried with joy
– Joyful. Life is now worth living.

The last response was made by a girl who is an orphan. More than half the teenage mothers thought that their lives had changed tremendously after delivery. They admitted that the amount of work had increased and that their social activities had been restricted. Many of them complained about financial problems and stated that they were now thinking of finding some means of earning a living. One mother in Morogoro was not happy with her baby because she had a premature delivery and the baby was still in the incubator two months later. During the first two weeks, she feared her baby because she was so small. She was afraid to breast-feed her. As a result, she had to squeeze milk out of her breasts into a cup, and then feed the baby with a spoon. The nurse in charge of the incubation ward said that such behaviour is common and that several girls try to run away from their children.

"It is not my intention to run away from the baby", one sad looking young mother told us. "It is very tedious to have to visit the baby every three hours to give him milk, as the rate of growth is too slow." "I am ashamed to show my baby to another person. It is too small", another girl in the incubation ward informed her mother.

All the teenage mothers were breast-feeding their babies but one out of four claimed that their milk was insufficient. They knew it because the children would suck for a short time and then start crying. During the night, the children would suck continuously for a long time but still cry. Asked what supplement they used to the breastmilk, they mentioned porridge and fruits, which were fed to babies at around three months, and in some cases even earlier. When asked whether they had any knowledge of the breast-feeding patterns to follow, most stated that the medical advice was to feed on demand. The girls commonly indicated that they had been taught at the clinics about what types of other food they should give their babies and when to start feeding. The nurses who monitored the babies' growth always reminded them about this. The girls remembered very well that they should give fruits (juices mostly) and porridge to the children at around three months and other kinds of food after six months.

The teenage mothers faced many physical, social and financial problems during pregnancy and delivery and while raising their children. As a result, about half of them indicated that they planned to have another baby only after four years. Five girls indicated that they wanted to have another baby only after five or more years, while one teenage mother commented that she was not ready to have another baby. This mother and her child were both suffering from tuberculosis and she was deeply troubled and moved by the severe pains they were experiencing. She worried about whether the child would survive and she feared giving birth to another baby with the same disease. One sixteen year old mother who had had a stillbirth did not think she would have another similar experience. Several girls indicated that they had made no decision about when to have

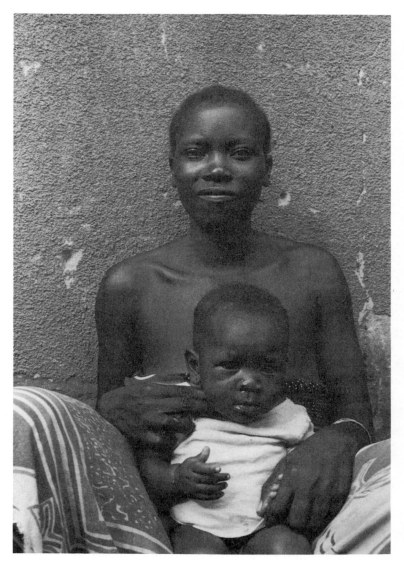

Many young mothers felt that their lives had changed tremendously after delivery, but in different ways, depending on whether they were married or not.
Photo: Sv.Å. Lorents Christensen, Bazaar Bildbyrå, Stockholm

another baby. It is the husband or his relatives who decide when another baby should be conceived. When they were asked about the number of children they wanted to have, four was the median number for most girls but some were not sure whether their husbands would agree to this or insist on more.

What next?

Many teenage mothers had earlier indicated that they were not willing to have more babies. We decided to find out about the preventive measures they planned to use. About eighty girls (66 per cent) had decided to use family planning services, but did not indicate the specific methods they would use. They were confident that they would be given guidance on the best methods at the clinics and they were aware that the nurses and doctors who offer services in these clinics are experts. The remaining girls listed several methods. Some mentioned abstinence, others local herbs and three mothers were undecided because of religious beliefs that prohibit family planning or because their community was against child spacing.

The mothers who were not in favour of using modern contraceptives gave several reasons why they disliked them. One teenage mother commented that they were tiresome to use. "One has to take a pill everyday, even when you don't have sex", she said. Another unmarried teenage mother feared that her parents and neighbours would misunderstand her and suspect her of being a prostitute. "When married women see me at the clinics, they will wonder why I need the pills. I have no husband or stable boy-friend." Another fourteen year old mother commented: "The question of giving contraceptives to teenagers is debatable in our society, because some people feel it will encourage prostitution or lead to serious reproductive problems in future."

Conclusion

This study has shown that teenagers do not receive adequate information about their reproductive health. The scanty information obtained from peers, mothers and close relatives is often conveyed piecemeal. Teenagers seem to lack knowledge of the safe period, appropriate age for safe pregnancy, and family planning methods and do not realize the consequences of having sexual relationships with boys and men; some of them think sexual contact is merely fun. We noticed that some of the expectant teenagers did not even realize that they were pregnant even after five months.

We also discovered in this study that expectant teenagers become disturbed and worried about their futures when they realize that they are pregnant, because in most cases the men responsible are not willing to marry them. They also fear the parents' reaction and feel ashamed of the pregnancy itself because of societal attitudes towards "out of wedlock" pregnancies.

10. What has the law got to do with it?

Magdalena Kamugisha Rwebangira

When I started legal practice in 1978, I went to court one day and this was the scene that met my eyes:

The courtroom was fully packed and not even standing room was available. In the dock sat a wretched mother who was absent-mindedly feeding her baby. "What has brought her to this court of justice?", people were asking. "That devil has killed her baby", was the answer. "This mother is a child herself", another shouted.

The accused mother could not have been more than seventeen years old. She looked lonely and miserable as she sat in the dock. It emerged later that when she gave birth to her first child, she was unable to take care of herself and the baby. The father of the child was nowhere to be found. She became so disturbed that in desperation, she killed the child. She considered the child to be the root cause of her suffering. On the advice of her counsel, she pleaded guilty. The court gave her a suspended sentence.

This particular case and several similar ones that came before the courts stimulated my interest and prompted me to look at the law and practice governing abortion and infanticide, with special reference to teenage girls.

State law has displaced many traditional systems for regulating fertility in adolescent girls with the unfortunate consequence that these moral controls have been weakened. The Penal Code covers abortion, rape and other related issues with a view to protecting women, especially the young, from the harmful effects of sexual activity.

The Tanzanian government passed *The Law of Marriage Act* (LMA) in 1971. Jurists, judges and academicians have hailed this as a milestone and as pioneering legislation in Commonwealth Africa, because it grants women legal equality with men.[1] This law gives women some civil rights in marriage and divorce. It sets the minimum marriage age at eighteen although this can be reduced for girls to fifteen with parental approval.[2] This minimum age can be lowered to fourteen for both boys and girls by court order if parents unreasonably withhold consent for the girls.[3] It is worth noting that the boy does not need parental consent to contract a valid marriage. The implication here is that the boy's undertaking in marriage is between himself and the state, even at the age of fourteen. However, a woman needs parental consent even at the age of seventeen. The same *Law of Marriage Act* states that, for a marriage to be considered valid, both the man and the woman must give their consent. The law does not consider bridewealth necessary for the establishment of a valid marriage. Section 41 of the Act states this in clear language. In this case, the *Law of Marriage Act* comes into direct conflict with customary law requirements for a valid marriage. This is because bridewealth is still an acknowledged part of the customary marriage ceremony in many, if not most communities.

My interest in undertaking the present study dates back to 1978 when I started legal practice. Almost all teenage girl suspects I met and sometimes defended in court had two features in common. Firstly, they were charged with infanticide; secondly, the baby had been their first. Many girls pleaded guilty on the advice of defence counsel and often received suspended sentences. By another coincidence, many of these girls had a nursing baby at their breasts or on their backs when they sat in the dock. This particular circumstance was often used as mitigation by defence counsel to show that the accused girl had since reformed and could be a useful citizen in the community if she were given another chance. The maximum sentence allowed by law for this offence is life im-

---

1. See Read, J.S., 1972, "A Milestone in the integration of Personal Laws: The New Law of Marriage and Divorce in Tanzania", *Journal of African Law*, (16, 1, 20. Also, Mwaikasu, R.J.A., 1982, *Family Law as a Vehicle for Improvement of the Status of African Women in Modern African States with particular reference to Tanzania Mainland*. LL M thesis, University of London.
2. Law of Marriage Act (LMA), 1971, p. 13 (1).
3. LMA, p. 13 (2).

prisonment. I have since wondered about the other options available to girls, besides having another baby.

I wanted to look at the right, or lack of it, to contraception, and also at the law and practice governing abortion and infanticide. I specifically wanted to focus on the interaction between teenage girls and the law in these three aspects. The general conceptual framework of the terms "contraception", "family planning", "abortion" and "infanticide" (unless otherwise explained in specific contexts) will here mean the following. *Contraception* refers to devices or substances aimed at preventing fertilization inside a woman's body. *Family planning* has been given many definitions depending on the purpose intended to be accomplished by its use, including child spacing, birth control, etc. In this chapter it will refer to those services intended to give women (and other members of the community) autonomy over their reproductive lives by entrusting them both with the authority to make decisions about their reproductive capacities and access to the information and services necessary for them to make informed choices. Abortion will mean the spontaneous or artificially induced termination of pregnancy before twenty-eight weeks of gestation.

The control of teenage reproduction has engaged the attention of many societies since precolonial times. Many communities in Tanzania, and indeed many African societies, had elaborate systems for regulating the fertility of adolescent girls. Modern state law has, in many cases, taken over, and consequently weakened these traditional controls. This state law includes the Penal Code; the *Law of Marriage Act,* 1971; the *Affiliation Ordinance* (Cap. 335); the National Education Act, 1978; the *Customary Law Declaration Order,* 1963, as well as community and court practice. All these norms taken together form the checks and balances in birth law.

The Penal Code creates offences which in one way or another affect teenagers in their reproductive role. By bringing abortion and other related offences under the Penal Code, the law aims at preventing commission thereof or assistance therein in terminating pregnancy, or causing the death of a live child within the first year of life. Likewise, penalties for other offences like rape, abduction of girls under sixteen, defilement of girls under fourteen, detention of women on premises or brothels, are seen as measures protecting women, especially the very young, from the harmful sexual proclivities of men.

The *Affiliation Ordinance* deals with rules of paternity for children born out of wedlock. There are two systems of law governing the affiliation of children in Tanzania. These are customary law as codified under the *Customary Law Declaration Order*, 1963, and the *Affiliation Ordinance* of 1949. The *Affiliation Ordinance* is based on English law. Under the *Customary Law Ordinance*, a mother's declaration regarding the paternity of a child is presumed to be true, unless the man can prove that he had no sexual intercourse with the mother of such a child (rule 183). It also makes provision for maintenance of such children by the fathers. This could serve as relief, particularly for teenage mothers who almost always have problems supporting themselves and their children. But under the *Affiliation Ordinance*, the burden of proof lies on the mother who has to prove that the man she has named is truly the father of her child(ren). A mother's declaration concerning the paternity of her child can be refuted by the named man.[4] Both these positions are only relevant if the parents are unmarried at the time of the child's birth. Neglect and desertion of children are criminal offences under the Penal Code.[5] It is an offence under the *National Education Act*, 1978, to cause a child between seven and thirteen years of age who is enrolled in school to drop out of such school before completion of the education for which he/she is enrolled.[6]

Given this legal position, how do teenage girls utilize the law? Similarly, how does Tanzanian society evoke the law to regulate adolescents' behaviour and ultimately their reproductive health? And how do teenagers interact with the law in their reproductive lives and roles in modern Tanzania? It has been said that *reproductive rights are so basic for women that the enjoyment of other rights depends on them.* Thus these reproductive rights and constraints

---

4. See Customary Law Declaration Order, 1963, rule 183. This differs from the provisions of the Affiliation Ordinance whereby the burden of proof is on the woman that it is the particular man who is responsible for the pregnancy. See also Rwezaura, B.A., "Tanzania: More protection for children", *Journal of Family Law*, 25, 261.
5. Penal Code, pp. 166, 167.
6. National Education Act, 1978, p. 35 and by-laws made by the Minister of Education under p. 35 (4).

must be placed within the context of other legal rights.

I adopted basic women's law methodology. This means I had to describe the law, understand how it interacts with particular women's lives and be able to explain why women end up in the position they are in, with a view to improving their legal and social position.[7]

The law constructs the social space within which people are allowed or not allowed to operate. Women's law, which is a feminist jurisprudence, argues that these laws are made mostly by men and are tailored for men's needs and experiences, thus ignoring and constraining women's lives. Women's law, therefore, examines how the law in its many facets affects women's lives, i.e., it takes women as a starting point.

It views birth law as a branch of women's law, and seeks to gather, systematize and analyse the many fragmented legal rules that specifically concern the creation and planning of new-born life.[8] It contends, among others that "if women are to have the possibility to plan their lives at all, self-determined pregnancy and birth are essential rights".[9]

I took the young women as a starting point, although this was not always possible. For one thing, identifying the girls who had interacted with the law but whose cases had already been decided was not easy. Often the girls had moved or returned to the rural areas after their frightening encounters with the law. Secondly, for ethical reasons, I could not gain access to the court records of those girls whose cases were still in progress. Consequently, I had to rely on traditional methods of investigation known as the "top to bottom" approach.

I collected my data by various methods, including a general survey of literature and public documents, interviews with public officials and community leaders, group discussions, and both structured and unstructured questionnaires.

I conducted the study in two regions of mainland Tanzania, namely Kagera and Dar es Salaam. Kagera is located in northwestern

---

7. Dahl, S.T., 1987, *Women's law. An Introduction to Feminist Jurisprudence.* Oslo: Norwegian University Press.
8. Ibid., p. 20.
9. Ibid., p. 106.

Tanzania. It shares borders with Uganda, Rwanda and Burundi. The region comprises five districts, Bukoba, Ngara, Karagwe, Muleba and Biharamulo. However, I concentrated my study on the regional and district headquarters of Bukoba district for reasons of transport, time and logistics. Bukoba district is served by one district court, one resident magistrate's court and twenty-two primary courts. The study was conducted in the district and resident magistrate's court. I selected this region because it is far from the centre of "modern" influence. It also has historical factors that are distinctive on the Tanzanian mainland, and similar only to the other interacustrine states of Bunyoro, Ankole, Toro in Uganda and Rwanda and Burundi. At independence, Bukoba had an elaborate semi-feudal social system with definite social classes. It had its own system of slavery under which mostly women were taken as slaves in exchange for favours from the king and various religious obligations.[10]

Premarital conception was strictly forbidden for both boys and girls. If such things occurred they resulted in forced marriages, in addition to several other penalties to "cleanse" the girl's family and appease the ancestors. If the girl could not name the father of an "illicit" pregnancy, she was killed by drowning with a big stone attached to her neck (*kumunaga omu kitatenga*).[11] All children had to be affiliated to a father. I felt it useful to see how much social change has affected attitudes and conduct towards teenage reproduction.

Dar es Salaam region comprises three districts, Ilala, Kinondoni and Temeke. They are served by three district courts – City, Kivukoni and Kisutu – which are designated for each of the districts although they are all located in the city centre within walking distance of each other. I chose Dar es Salaam because it is the centre of political, legal,

---

10. Reining P., 1967, *The Haya; An Agrarian System of a Sedetary People.* Ph. D thesis University of Chicago.
Swantz, M., 1985, *Women in Development: A Creative Role Denied? The Case of Tanzania.* London: C. Hurst & Company.
Larsson, B., 1991, *Conversion to the Greater Freedom: Women, Church and Social Change in North-Western Tanzania under Colonial Rule.* Ph.D Thesis University of Uppsala.
11. Oral accounts from the author's grandmothers and other relatives.

Family planning session for those who are married. Resentment towards single women's sexuality is deeply rooted in the community.
Daily News, Dar es Salaam

economic and social activity in the country. It is a symbol of modernity and has a concentration of the best educated people in Tanzania. Its cosmopolitan nature makes its inhabitants less tied by traditional social constraints. Also, it is the de facto capital of Tanzania, possessing most institutional headquarters, so that decision-makers are accessible for interview.

Contraception, a sensitive issue

The distribution of contraceptives and other related services is one strategy of Tanzania's Ministry of Health on family planning, according to the Ministry's Plan of Operations, 1989–93. Family planning facilities have a long history in the city of Dar es Salaam, dating back to 1959, when the Family Planning Association of Dar es Salaam was founded. This later became a national organisation in 1967 and changed its name to the Family Planning Association of Tanzania (UMATI), and has catered to the whole country since

1972, mainly at regional hospitals.[12] Family planning has been provided as a component of comprehensive Maternal and Child Health (MCH) services since 1974.[13]

Although in clause 4, UMATI's constitution gives directives on guidance to adolescents in preparation for their future role as parents, in practice it excludes them from contraceptive services. Its emphasis has been on family-life education and youth counselling, in an effort to promote young people's awareness of their sexuality and of human reproduction. However, efforts to introduce family life education in schools – the label signifies sex education – have met with sustained resistance from Tanzania's diverse society.[14] This was evident at a seminar on population and development for members of parliament held in Arusha in May 1984, where members of parliament categorically rejected the government's plan to introduce family-life education in schools.[15] This reluctance partly explains why young unmarried girls have been practically excluded from UMATI's services, although there has never been a law prohibiting UMATI from extending its contraceptive services to unmarried adolescents. Likewise, it could be said that the government, although supporting the family planning initiative, remained in the background and left UMATI to carry out its activities as a private and voluntary organisation until 1974 when the Ministry of Health introduced family planning services at Mother and Child Health Clinics. Even then, the Ministry of Health did not establish a specific unit for this purpose until 1988 when a National Family Planning arm was introduced.

---

12. Mwateba, R., 1989, "UMATI's Contribution in Career Guidance and Counselling to Teenage Mother's". A Paper presented at Tanzania Media Women (TAMWA)'s Day of Action on 26th May 1989 at Goethe Institute, Dar es Salam.
13. See Tanzania Ministry of Health, Plan of Operations 1989–93.
14. Mazrui, A. A., 1986, *The Africans: A Triple Heritage*. Little Brown and Company, Boston, USA.
15. Olekambainei, P., 1990, "Problems leading to school drop-outs among the Youths in Tanzania (especially girls)". Paper presented at training workshop for Teenage Girls and Reproductive Health Project, Bahari Beach Hotel, 30 July–3 August. In 1992, a pilot Family Life Education (FLE) programme was introduced in a number of selected schools, after a successful campaign led by the Ministry of Education.

It would appear that both government and UMATI were exercising self-restraint in view of the sensitivity of the subject. Indeed, the debate on the amendment of the *Employment Ordinance* to include maternity benefits for both married and unmarried women revealed that there was widespread concern that the extension of these benefits to unmarried women would encourage promiscuity and prostitution. Hence, resentment towards single women's sexuality is deeply rooted in the community. Arguably, this tendency stems from the patriarchal desire to control women's sexuality and fertility. Young women's and school girls' use of family planning services stood little, if any, chance of acceptance. A backlash that could threaten the entire family planning programme was probably feared. Thus the registration card for UMATI required particulars about "the husband", effectively eliminating the majority of its potential unmarried teenage women clients.

The female population in the country, aged fifteen to nineteen years, was 5 per cent in 1978, and the same pattern was observed in 1988. Only 35 per cent of teenagers are married and hence theoretically eligible for UMATI services.[16] The new initiative as spelt out in the Ministry of Health's policy paper and practice on family planning gives cause for optimism. In terms of policy, it states that:

the government endorses the principle enshrined in the World Population Plan of Action that all men and women have the right freely and responsibly to decide the number and spacing of their children, and the right to information, education and means to do so.[17]

One notes here that the principle is broad enough to include adolescent girls, but is susceptible to differing interpretations. As for eligibility for service, the policy paper states in its service provision

---

16. The United Republic of Tanzania, 1978 Population Census Report and 1988 Population Census: Preliminary Report. Dar es Salaam, Bureau of Statistics, Ministry of Finance, Economic Affairs and Planning.
17. Ministry of Health, 1989, *"Plan of Operations 1989–93"*. Dar es Salaam, Tanzania, p. 57.

guidelines that any adult person, male or female, is eligible. In practice, the National Family Planning Project of the Ministry of Health has since 1988 interpreted "an adult person" to mean anyone who has reached puberty!

Technically this is debatable, as an adult person under the constitution is one who has attained the age of eighteen years. However, what difference does it make if a person who is technically a minor participates in full community life either through marriage or sexuality, circumstances which put him/her at greater risk than his/her adult counterparts? A study conducted in three regions of Tanzania revealed that overall, about 61 per cent of adolescent boys and about 40 per cent of adolescent girls engage in sexual intercourse, and that of these over 81 per cent of boys and 82 per cent of girls do so at least once a week. The age at which sexual activity begins among adolescents was found to be between fourteen and fifteen years.[18]

Thus it would appear that the impediment is not state law, but cultural and religious attitudes about morality. It was noted during the survey of the family planning clinics that the recent AIDS control initiative has been more successful in getting the clinics and the youth, especially school girls, to talk to each other, but only, as one counsellor noted, "provided they do not come in school uniforms". In fact, young girls, let alone schoolgirls, were rarely seen at the clinics even though a sixteen year old girl attired in a traditional *khanga* can easily pass for twenty or older.

Unwanted pregnancies

The truth remains that adolescent girls are not given any guidance on contraception. This neglect leads to unwanted pregnancies. During my study, five pregnant teenage girls in Kinondoni district revealed that they were faced with rejection, banishment from home, illegal abortions and, of course, expulsion from school.[19] One

---

18. Kamuzora, C. L., 1985, "Adolecent Sexuality, Consequences and Knowledge of Contraception and Associated Factors". A paper presented.
19. Case studies of Kashinje, Asha, Farida and Mercy, all of Konondoni district.

was sent to live with her uncle, one with her grandmother, still another was sent to live with her divorced mother, another one to the rural area where her parents lived, and the last got married to the father of the child after delivery. Other case studies of court proceedings revealed that pregnancy was the major cause of suicide attempts among teenage girls. Newspaper accounts during the research period gave pregnancy and forced marriage as the leading cause of the reported cases of suicide.[20] Thus unavailability of family planning services to the youth particularly discriminates against girls, because they are the ones most affected by unwanted pregnancies. Studies undertaken in 1980 and 1984 by other researchers show that pregnancy was the number one cause of school drop-outs for girls.[21] Overall, the incidence of pregnancy among adolescent girls both in and out of school is estimated at 13.2 per cent in Tanzania.[22]

The social environment of illegal abortion

Despite the law, my study has confirmed that abortions on request do take place in both private and public hospitals. The study on "Women, Law and Population" conducted in Dar es Salaam and Morogoro regions concluded that "an average of sixty abortions were carried out in the Dar es Salaam region, and five in the Morogoro region every week".[23] The individual doctors interviewed in Dar es Salaam for the present study estimated that two to three

20. See *Daily News*, 10 June 1992, "Teach Family Planning in Schools, Women say". The Magogoni Creek incident, reported in *Daily News*, 28 October 1991, "Suicide Woman not identified".
21. Siwale, T., quoted in Mwateba ibid. at p. 4.
Mbunda W., 1984, "Descriptive Study for Dar es Salaam Social Misfits". Chama cha Uzazi na Malezi Bora Tanzania (UMATI) referred in Mwateba ibid reference.
22. Urassa, E. J. N., 1990, "Reproductive Disorders Associated with Teenage Pregnancy and Childbirth". A paper presented at a Training Workshop for Teenage Girls Reproductive Health Study Group at Dar es Salaam Bahari Beach Hotel 30 July–3 August 1990.
23. Kapinga, W. B. L. and Gondwe, Z. S., September, 1991, "Family Planning in Tanzania", in *Law, Women and Population Studies in Tanzania*, pp. 44–50. Dar es Salaam UNFPA/Faculty of Law, University of Dar es Salaam.

illegal but safe abortions per day took place at Muhimbili Medical Centre alone. Many felt these figures are gross underestimates. They were also of the unanimous view that the number of safe abortions that occurred illegally in the hospitals exceeded cases of complications from unsafe illegal abortions. The number of safe illegal abortions is estimated at eight to ten per day in each private clinic. Their availability depends on the individual's ability to pay and/or good connections with doctor(s).

Even had permission to examine hospital records been granted, which it was not, it would have been difficult to obtain accurate and reliable data on actual abortions that take place in hospitals and clinics because of their illegality. Such abortions are not likely to be recorded in public hospitals. If they are, they may be recorded as incomplete, septic, inevitable, D & C, etc., implying that the process was commenced outside the hospital, in order to justify the medical procedure. The same applies to private clinics. The figures are probably an underestimate due to the illegal nature of the actions. Much, therefore, goes unrecorded.

In both Kagera and Dar es Salaam regions, herbal abortionists, and the methods they use, were known of in the women's community. Doctors said they were familiar with some of these methods from the insertions they find in the wombs of the patients who present with complications from backstreet abortions. In Dar es Salaam, insertions of cassava leaves were said to be the most common. In Kagera, it was said to be a secret herbal concoction known only to the herbalist. This causes severe bleeding leading to the expulsion of the foetus. This method is reportedly practised in Dar es Salaam, but to a lesser degree. In Bukoba, it was reported that bones and other sharp instruments were used, including copper wires and radio batteries.

Within the women's community these services are seen as socially useful and legitimate. These sentiments may explain why there seems to be an unspoken conspiracy to protect illegal practitioners. The victims of their practices would rather die than reveal the identity of their "doctors" and many do actually die.[24] Extracting confessions is not the legitimate business of doctors, but sometimes

---

24. Urassa, E. J. N., ibid. p. 9

it is necessary for them to determine the most efficient treatment required to save the life of a patient. At Bukoba Regional Government Hospital in Kagera, the doctors seem to do more than that. There confession is very often a precondition for treatment of the effects of illegal abortion. During the research period a number of girls who died at the hospital were suspected of being victims of such circumstances. One girl had been a secondary school boarder. She was not feeling well and asked permission to go home. At home she continued to have fevers and abdominal pain (*ekijoka*), according to her mother.

She had no AIDS symptoms. So I decided to bring her to a big hospital. She did not get better, in fact she got worse. The doctors asked her endless questions but nothing helped. She stopped eating. She did not swallow anything for two days, then she vomited once and died. My daughter suffered a lot. But it was not AIDS (ti kiuka).

According to hospital personnel, the girl was a septic abortion case who deceived her mother and pretended not to know what was wrong with her. She was offered treatment, provided that she admitted her action and named the person who had assisted her to procure the abortion, but she declined.

While in the hospital, her mother started to look for traditional herbs. She gave her *enkaka*, a thorny, thick green herb which has a bitter taste. Locally it is believed to be used in the making of modern quinine. The doctors panicked when she vomited a thick green solution just before she died, fearing suicide or poisoning. The mother, feeling guilty that she might have unwittingly hastened her daughter's death, confessed that she had secretly administered the *enkaka* to cure the abdominal pain. Would this honest and bold confession have saved the girl's life if it had been made earlier? Probably not, but the intended message for other girls and relatives was that it would. What legitimacy do such messages have? As long as abortion is illegal, the girl, the abortionist(s) and the suppliers of abortion instruments can be prosecuted. By refusing to name her facilitator(s), the girl was not only protecting her "doctor" (most of them are women), but also herself from possible prosecution, as well as the integrity of her family. But the hospital's lack of enthusiasm about treating patients who do not confess to septic abortions is clearly illegal, and also unethical, because the girl's life was obviously in danger. How do teenage girls fare in all this?

Abortion

As far as abortion is concerned, it is illegal under the Penal Code and is punishable by imprisonment for fourteen years for the abortionist, seven years for the woman herself, and three years for any person supplying drugs or instruments to procure abortion. Thus Tanzania falls into that minority group of countries where abortion is available only to save the mother's life. By 1987, this kind of law affected about 13 per cent of the world's population, most of them in sub-Saharan Africa.[25]

The term "abortion" in the legal context usually refers to induced abortion. It has been the subject of controversy internationally. Both pro-abortion, and especially anti-abortion groups, have been actively mobilizing people in the West as well as in the Third World countries to support their respective causes. In developing countries where this life/choice debate has yet to take root, efforts have been made to ensure that liberal views never gain political as well as legal ground. The anti-abortion lobby has, for example, been active in Zambia although that country finally succeeded in liberalizing its abortion law.

In Tanzania, the debate has, at least for now, been avoided. Nonetheless, groups like "The Association for the Rights of the Unborn", drawing membership from institutions of higher learning and other elite sections of society, are evidence that victory would be difficult.[26] The "born" children, however, have not received such compassion from the same quarters.

---

25. Chikanza, I. and Chinamora, W., 1987, "Abortion in Zimbabwe: A Medico – Legal Problem", in Armstrong A. and W. Ncube, *Women and Law in Southern Africa*, pp. 237–251, Zimbabwe Publishing House, Harare, Zimbabwe.

26. A number of academic members of staff at the Faculty of Law, University of Dar es Salaam, for example, belong to the association in Tanzania.

Doctors' and nurses' opinions on teenage girls and abortion

Fifteen doctors and nurses involved in abortion cases answered my questionnaire. I asked them on what grounds they would consider abortion for an adult woman under the present law. Medical grounds were the reason given by an overwhelming majority. The same question was put to them with regard to teenagers, and then two-thirds said they would proceed on medical grounds. Prodded further on teenagers specifically, only one-third said they would consider abortion on social grounds, and then only as second and third in significance. One out of six said they would consider it on grounds of AIDS, and the figure was the same for "no way". The same doctors were also asked about the frequency of cases of teenagers with complications from induced illegal abortions – two-thirds of them said there were one to ten per month, and one-sixth stated over forty per month. It was noted that the majority of doctors in the first category were based in a public hospital, while those in the second, though few in number, worked in private hospitals, implying that private hospitals conduct more abortions.

Asked of their experience with the health hazards affecting teenage girls after illegal abortions, a great majority ranked infertility in the first and second place, and two-thirds mentioned death as in the first three places. Other hazards mentioned included regular repeat abortions, removal of the uterus, severe bleeding and infection.

Asked if it was cheaper to treat abortion on request than deal with the complications from illegal abortions, 100 per cent said yes. The reasons given were:
– illegal abortion might cost somebody her life
– uterus can be perforated
– expensive to treat (many antibiotics)
– there are experts to perform safe abortions
– technically it is simpler to induce an abortion, it takes a
  few minutes and needs no admission except resting for two to
  three hours.

As to what reasons seekers of safe illegal abortions give for their requests, the answers given are ranked in the following order; school, economic reasons, shame and disputed paternity.

Regarding the choice of persons to accompany teenage girls

seeking legal safe abortions, boy-friends were selected by 50 per cent, parents, relatives (aunts and sisters), spouses and friends were chosen by a third. Guardians and "nobody" were mentioned by none of them. This means that teenagers are always accompanied by someone to plead on their behalf for a safe abortion. In practice, this eliminates the majority of those whose parents do not have personal access to a doctor. Coincidentally, the traditional birth attendants in Kagera held the same view. With regard to those seeking illegal but safe abortions, parents and boy-friends came first with two-thirds of the girls selecting them; one-third had "nobody"; spouse, relatives, guardians and friends were ranked in the last place with only one out of six mentioning them.

In the search for treatment for complications arising from illegally induced abortions, parents topped the list. They were the first and second choice for an overwhelming majority; relatives came next being mentioned by the same percentage but ranked second and third. Friends were preferred by one-third and "nobody" by one out of six. Spouses were not selected by any.

In summary, doctors interviewed in both Dar es Salaam and Kagera regions said schooling was the first and foremost reason given by teenage girls seeking to terminate pregnancies illegally but safely. Although they agreed that the majority of seekers after safe abortion are adult women, adolescents comprise the majority of those whom they treated for often horrifying and sometimes fatal complications following illegally induced abortions. This view was unanimous among the doctors from the public hospitals. In the private hospitals it was said that the majority of people seeking safe illegal abortions were adult women and the adolescent girls were just average.

As the discussion above shows, parents of adolescent girls were often involved in the search for safe illegal abortions for their daughters. Boy-friends came in third after parents, sisters and aunts. Boy-friends mostly utilized private clinics, while parents generally used hospitals. Doctors interviewed described the latter as "genuine cases" of hardship. Some of the teenage girls who had had backstreet abortions took themselves to the public hospitals in critical condition. Of most assistance in these cases were the parents. Boy-friends did not feature. What this means is that services for the termination of pregnancy are confined to those who can afford to pay for them or who have connections with doctors in public hospitals. Given this position, should we be debating the morality of legalizing abortion? Can we continue to play innocent to the detriment of those who have neither the money nor the connections necessary to obtain a safe abortion? This study shows that teenage girls comprise the majority of those who lack such resources.

The case for legalizing abortion

I also asked doctors, nurses and prosecutors whether abortion should be legalized. Their responses varied. All doctors in the Kagera as well as the Dar es Salaam region unanimously thought that it should be legalized. The nurses' responses were qualified. Medically they agreed that it would be better and cheaper to deal with abortion but they thought that abortion was morally wrong. They were concerned about its effect on morality and lamented the young girls' greedy pursuit of rich men, etc. The prosecutors in effect did not think that the law was the problem because in practice there are very few prosecutions. Women prosecutors' concerns were similar to those of the nurses, although they did not object if legalization gave women more freedom.

Those who supported legalization gave the following reasons in order of highest frequency:
– may cost somebody's life
– uterus can be perforated when abortion is performed
   by inexperienced people
– expensive to treat (e.g., use of a lot of antibiotics)
– does not need admission, only rest for two to three hours
– permanent damage like infertility and habitual abortion
   can result.

It was noted that these answers, when put together, are identical to the answer on complications. Most filled "same as No 5" or "as above" in the questionnaire. As mentioned above, the prosecutors thought legalization was unnecessary because prosecutions for abortion were very rare.

Between 1989 and 1991, there had been only six prosecutions

related to abortion in Dar es Salaam, three for child destruction and three for abortion. In all six cases, the accused were teenage girls. There was only one recorded prosecution for concealment of birth in 1988 in Bukoba resident magistrates' court and the accused was a teenage girl. There were reports in the public media of medical practitioners being prosecuted for performing abortions when such act resulted in death. According to one article, a nurse and a rural medical aid at a health centre in Kizinda village, Kakonko ward in Kigoma region, gave the deceased an unspecified number of drugs and then pulled out the foetus by hand, thus tearing apart her intestines and the foetus which caused her instant death. The deceased, Tracksea Kiize, was nineteen years old.[27]

Another case was of a Dodoma doctor who allegedly single-handedly performed a clandestine abortion on his friend's wife in his office, and she died from excessive bleeding. The doctor reportedly went public with the story and gave himself up to the police. This was related by prosecutors at Kisutu court and many people remembered the story which had been reported in the papers. Apparently, when abortion is illegal, even medical doctors can perform unsafe abortions!

The Law, Women and Population Studies Project also encountered the same view of morality. About 87 per cent of the interviewees were against voluntary abortion and the liberalization of abortion laws on grounds of morality.[28] Other health providers in the National Family Planning arm of the Ministry of Health thought legalizing abortion would not solve the problem. One doctor in that section pointed out that the strain that this would place on the health services system would be overwhelming. The gynaecology and obstetrics doctors disagree. Liberalizing the abortion law is one thing, getting somebody willing to reform the law is another. If this unwilling attitude prevails, we will not progress far from where we are today. Accounts from Zambia where abortion is now legal, talk of long queues for abortion in government hospitals.[29] In any case,

---

27 *Daily News*, 15 November 1990, p. 3.
28 Kapinga, W. B. L. and Gondwe, Z. S., 1991 ibid.
29 Jacobson, J., July 1990, "The Global Politics of Abortion", *World Watch* paper No. 97.

nobody has ever done a cost-benefit analysis of the two situations in Tanzania; namely handling abortions safely on request or treating abortion complications. Such analysis and a more systematic survey of the social aspects of abortion would go far to build the case for or against legalized abortion. At least we would begin to obtain more accurate statistics on the magnitude of the problem, and that would make a lot of difference.

I presented some of these findings at the second SAREC (Swedish Agency for Research Cooperation with Developing Countries) workshop at Muhimbili Medical Centre in April 1991 and these were reported in the *Daily News* of 9 April 1992. Several responses were made in the letter columns, commenting on legalized abortion.[30] This was a positive development because the whole idea behind the exercise was to stimulate public debate on the issue.

The law and infanticide

The term *infanticide* refers to an offence in law whereby a baby is killed by its mother shortly after its birth. Under Tanzanian law the period of imprisonment is twelve months. It is also called baby dumping. It is an offence under the Penal Code, p. 199 of which states:

Where a woman by any wilful act or omission causes the death of a child, being a child under the age of twelve months, but at the time of the act or omission she had not fully recovered from the effect of giving birth to such child, and by reason thereof, or by reason of the effect of lactation consequent upon the birth of her child, the balance of her mind was then disturbed, she shall, not withstanding that the circumstances were such that but for this section the offence would have amounted to murder, be guilty of the offence termed "infanticide" and may for such offence be dealt with and punished as if she had been guilty of the offence of manslaughter of such child.

---

30. See *Sunday News*, 31 May 1992 (legalize abortion for schoolgirls); 12 July 1992 (anonymous); 6 September 1992 (abortion); 20 September 1992 (abortion opium of sex maniacs, don't legalize murder).

A child is deemed to be a person capable of being killed when it has been born alive, whether it has breathed or not, whether it has independent circulation or not, and whether the navel-string is severed or not (s. 204). Briefly, this is the viability test. The only exception the Code allows for lawful termination is when it is necessary to preserve the life of a mother.[31]

The offence of manslaughter is committed by the unlawful killing of another person and is punishable by life imprisonment (p. 195). Murder, on the other hand, is punishable by death sentence (p. 196).

The decline in infanticide prosecutions during the 1980s is evidenced by the scarcity of cases in the high court registries in the Dar es Salaam as well as Kagera regions. One explanation given by prosecutors in both regions is that there has been a tendency not to issue permits for the prosecution of abortion and infanticide cases. Many interviewees attributed the decline in infanticide incidence to the increase in illegal abortions. Between 1983 and 1990, only fourteen women were charged with infanticide in the Dar es Salaam High Court. Three of these women were adults (21.1 per cent) and the remaining eleven (78.6 per cent) were teenagers.

From 1983 to 1990 the average age of women charged with infanticide in Dar es Salaam was eighteen years, who were thus teenagers. In Kagera, there seems to be a valid percentage of 55 per cent, perhaps reflecting the lower economic status of women in rural areas. The average age is 21.1 years. The average number of cases per year is about 0.7, and the number of cases is less and the prevalence lower in Kagera (rural) than in the city (Dar es Salaam), although one case in Dar es Salaam originated from the coast region (Rufiji) which is also rural. One of the accused women in Kagera was a nun from a rural convent.

---

31. Penal Code, p. 204.

The sociology of the crime

The cause of death was dumping the baby in a pit latrine in fifteen of the nineteen cases in both regions. All except two took place in urban areas. In exceptional cases, death was caused by abandonment of the child when it was two months old. Another mother left the newborn child on a banana farm. In yet another, a five month old baby was suffocated to death with its mother's breast. In the remaining case, the accused was a nun. The case was withdrawn on the advice of the Director of Public Prosecutions (DPP) as he is entitled to do under the law.

With the exception of the abandonment case, all these exceptional cases occurred in Kagera. Cultural practices may be indicated here. However, some of those who used a pit latrine to dispose of their babies in Dar es Salaam were also from Kagera.[32] Moreover, not all rural families have the luxury of a pit latrine. Looking at these facts, one can easily gain the impression that there are no modern toilets in Tanzania. But if we recall the discussion on middle-class parental involvement in illegal abortions, the class nature of these two last-resort methods of birth control or disposing of an unwanted child, is obvious.

The sex of the child did not seem to matter. Indeed, this particular detail was rarely given. Out of the nineteen cases, the child's gender was mentioned in the four cases that did not involve dumping in a pit latrine. One of these (suffocated by breast), was a girl and the remaining three were boys.

The circumstances of birth were such that in all recorded cases in the study, the conditions of pregnancy were concealed and if detected, denied. They were all first pregnancies and were out of wedlock. In one case, the woman got married when she was seven months pregnant but pretended she had conceived immediately after marriage. She delivered after two months, and threw the baby in the pit latrine. She deceived everybody and sent for distant relatives, complaining about her stomach problems and the late arrival of her menses. Her action was established by medical

---

32. See, *DSM Criminal Sessions Case No 86/86 R v Adventina Ganus.*

evidence after the discovery of the baby's body.[33] Another feature common to all cases was that the girls were alone when they delivered and also when they disposed of the babies.

The common defence in six out of the nineteen cases was denial, and not knowing that they were in labour in the rest of the cases. They claimed that the act was accidental as they thought they were only obeying a call of nature. It has been said that these defences were possibly honest but mistaken. Many adult women would agree that it is possible to make this mistake, especially when it is your first birth and you are uninformed.[34]

On the other hand, teenagers are under greater pressure to control fertility than adult women. There are socio-economic and cultural disadvantages for unmarried teenage mothers.[35] The teenage years are also the time to invest in education. Although none of the infanticide "delinquents" were students (these know better to abort early), they may well have wanted marriage, with its expected social and economic security. So there is the opportunity cost too. Their occupations ranged from "housegirl" (*ayah*) (2), to convent nun (1), to housewives (2), and the rest were single and unattached. All these women had rural backgrounds. In all the Dar es Salaam cases, the women had moved from rural areas to the city. In Kagera region, three out of five culprits committed the offence in the village and were apprehended there. The other two had come to the regional town (Bukoba) to seek employment after falling pregnant.

In all cases, the community acted in unison but only after the act. The latrines were smashed amid much fanfare. Sometimes the accused women were beaten by other women before being rescued by the police. But this righteousness was nowhere to be seen when the young woman was contemplating her future. Those who tried to keep the baby found themselves helpless so that they gave up. Most knew very little of what was about to happen to them, even during pregnancy, with regard to giving birth and/or raising the baby. The

---

33. Ibid.
34. Migiro, R., 1990, "Women and Criminal Law in Tanzania". Working Papers in *Women's Law* No.34. University of Oslo.
35. Mc Gee, E., 1987, *Too little, Too Late. Services for Teenage Parents*. A Working Paper from the Ford Foundation, 1987. New York, USA.

following is a case study of an adolescent girl who tried to gain her economic independence, raise her baby and gain social autonomy but ended up abandoning the baby and being charged with infanticide.

"It was not easy"

The girl was eighteen years old. When seven months pregnant, she left her home village in Mbeya and came to Dar es Salaam. In her own words, she had been invited by her boy-friend whom she had known sometime back when he worked in her home town. The boy-friend received her in Dar es Salaam and put her up in a guest house. Thereafter, the man disappeared from the scene. The girl stayed in the guest house and literally became a prostitute, going to discos, and dating men from all races and walks of life until she delivered.

It was apparent to her and her landlords that there was a problem of residence given her new role as a mother. She approached an old woman who owned rental premises in the vicinity. The old woman sympathized with her and offered her free accommodation in the outer rooms (*uani*). According to the girl, the old woman, who also lived on the premises in another room, was supposed to breast-feed the baby for her for a consideration, because "she had no milk herself". In the meantime she resumed her pre-delivery life as a prostitute. She was hardly at home but she visited when her busy schedule allowed. The existence of the baby was not mentioned to any of her associates.

In due course she received information from home that her sister was sick. She started making private arrangements to go home. In the meantime the baby fell sick. On the fateful day she stayed at home, which was unusual, with her sick child. The baby boy, two months old, was suffering from diarrhoea. At the end of the day she packed her bag and left for her home village to see her sister. She left the baby alone in her room. The baby died later that evening. The cause of death was diagnosed as HUNGER.

The old woman was arrested, of course. Where was the mother of the deceased? Under what arrangements had the mother been living in the house? Was the old woman ever paid to look after the baby? Did she take over or make the mother believe that she was taking over her parental responsibilities towards the child? The answer was no to all the questions. The old woman was only being helpful. She had never been demanded to be paid. Apparently, this was the most important point of law to be decided before she was released from liability, according to the girl's defence counsel. Anyway, the mother had not breast-fed the baby, or given any money to buy tinned milk for him.

The girl returned after three weeks. She was arrested as she alighted from the bus to Dar es Salaam. On the way, she was given the bad news and a lot of advice about what she should have done. Her initial response is reported to have been, "It was not easy".[36]

Some reflections

My purpose was to find out how the law interacts with the reproductive health of teenage girls. It was revealed that the law actually does interfere with their reproductive health either actively or by omission. With regard to contraception, although there is no state law to restrain girls' access to contraception, the living law of the community was found to interfere in practice. As to abortion, the umbrella of illegality under which it occurs, allows so much activity to go unrecorded and, therefore, makes monitoring of the practice speculative. Infanticide was seen as declining in the city where unsafe and safe abortions are rising, and as mostly affecting girls from among the rural poor.

The UN Convention on the Elimination of All Forms of Discrimination Against Women interprets access to healthcare as including family planning services and information (Articles 12(a) and 14(2)). The United Republic of Tanzania ratified this convention in August 1985. Although such services have not been embodied wholesale in domestic legislation, the policy paper on family planning mentioned above is an indication that the government is at least prepared to take "appropriate measures" to face up to the challenge.

---

36. See R.v Zainabu Mwinuka, DSM Criminal Sessions Case No 62/88. Also TLC/145/RHC/911.

Conclusions

Zubeida Tumbo-Masabo

In the past, the transition from childhood to womanhood was immediate and direct, and menarche was a sign of initiation and readiness to marry. There was no adolescence, no time to fall into reveries, no moratorium for psycho-social maturation, no ideas about training and qualifying for jobs. All these came with the introduction of mandatory schooling. With prolonged education and better earning opportunities the marital age increased. Hence, a gap between childhood and adulthood emerged. While girls used to be regarded as marriageable and ready to prove their fertility, they are nowadays expected to remain virgins for years after menarche. No wonder that girls soon find themselves trapped and torn between customary expectations and the claims of modernization; left in a vacuum between childhood and womanhood, hitherto unknown in sub-Saharan Africa. The initiation rites that used to prepare them as gendered and sexual beings have become obsolete, and the emergence of sexuality as a bio-physiological drive has not been followed by any concrete instructions on how to cope with it. Societies that had been open but strict about sexuality, became loose and silent, hiding and making a taboo of the topic.

It is evident in most chapters of this book that the teenage girl is overburdened, caught between cross pressures and double messages. She is supposed to decipher a symbolic language that she is not always familiar with, and which sometimes does not make sense to her. She is then expected to practise what she has learned in her real life. As soon as she reaches puberty it is still taken for granted that she will control herself, while a boy is given time to keep on growing into a mature man. The public attitude is more tolerant of a man's irresponsible behaviour, but has many misgivings about a woman's slightest mistake.

By and large, teenage girls harvest the fruit of men's desire, the bitter fruit of early and unwanted pregnancies and children abandoned by their fathers. The girls are condemned by the community,

Unleashed potential, powerful and concentrated...
Daily News, Dar es Salaam

expelled from school and have to face the disappointment of their
parents. Societies all over the world have sacrificed their daughters
for the sake of controlling the rules of marriage and the affiliation
of offspring. While the whole reproductive order has been undermined by change, it appears absurd, not to say unfair, to place the
blame upon young girls. The pubescent girls who once played such

important roles in the circulation of bridewealth, today seem to embody the loss of old values, and are punished for that.

The demand made of female teenagers to remain virgins in a culture of virile men who are brought up to feel superior to women, diverts moral responsibility from men. Teenage girls are susceptible to harassment by men and boys, at the same time as they have to face punishment from older women.

In the educational system, a girl bears all the burden of premature pregnancy. She is expelled from school and sometimes also from home. She is expected to fend for herself and the unborn baby without any means of survival. The father of the baby, on the other hand, who usually denies the paternity and does not give any support to the mother and child, is left to lead his life as if nothing has happened.

This "young woman", who sometimes is not older than fourteen years, seeks her livelihood through associations with men. She is then exploited further by men who use her for sexual pleasure without caring for her.

Teenage girls are now on the international agenda and given priority as an issue. For years they have been viewed through the neutral lens of "reproductive health"–an umbrella term not only signifying the absence of sexually transmitted diseases, HIV/AIDS, high-risk pregnancies, abortions, low birth weight, etc., but also implying additional goals such as "safe motherhood" and re-productive well-being. In this manner, the regeneration of life was subsumed under a medical concept, health. What once occurred in the West was repeated in Africa; a moral order was replaced by a scientific biomedical system, the priest and the shamans gave away to the doctors.

Recently, a new concept has been added, namely *sexual health*. The twin concepts, sexual and reproductive health, mark the distinction between sexual relationships that do not aim at child-bearing and those that have procreation as their aim. The new concept, sexual health, is geared to adolescents and to the recognition of the sexually active period before marriage.

The concepts are used in a very broad sense. Sexual health refers to "psychosexual development, sexuality, sex roles, family life and human relationships. Sexuality is seen as a positive force in peoples' lives, having an intrinsic value, not necessarily connected to reproduction" (SIDA Health Division, 1994).

The dividing line between intercourse for lust and for procreation has been made possible by modern contraceptives. However, the issues stretch far beyond medical technologies and what is meant by "health". The SIDA paper that we have quoted rightly states, that "reproduction in the broadest sense includes medical, social, psychosocial and cultural aspects". The time is ripe to discuss the issues involved in depth. These issues are not primarily medical, but have to do with what sexuality means to people, how it is culturally defined, how women and men understand themselves and their mutual relationships.

The lack of meaningful and open cultural dialogue between all those who are involved in promoting "health" and/or defending the moral order has obstructed problem solving. The teenage girl has been a symbolic battlefield between a bio-medical and socio-cultural view of man, she has been torn between an individualistic and collectivistic worldview. Instead of analysing the complex external transformations and the changing meaning of phenomena that were taken for granted, the blame has been placed on teenage girls, as if they were the core of the problem. It can hardly be said that the girls themselves invented these changes, yet they are left to bear the costs.

It is time to start talking about things that are real to all of us. We have to take into account the cultural meanings attached to sexuality and gendered relationships but also be concrete and practical in assisting the adolescents. We need to gain a better understanding about what sexuality, gender, family, and having children means to us, and the meaning all these have for cultures with different but universally changing designs for life. There might be values that we could agree about; personhood and the bodily integrity of women, respect for sexual diversity and gender equality.

There is a need to educate both girls and boys in a straightforward manner before they reach puberty. They should be taught about their bodies and how to manage fertility through discussion rather than by rote. And those who fall pregnant should be helped to manage their lives socially and economically through counselling and self-help groups which bring mothers and fathers together and guide them towards responsible parenthood. Ways should also be sought to help teenage mothers who have not completed their education to enable them to do so and, if possible, help them to get employment.

Moreover, by using government machinery, communities should be encouraged to abandon traditions which are detrimental to the well-being of teenage girls, such as early marriage and motherhood. Also, responsible fatherhood should be emphasized in the initiation of boys, as responsible motherhood is in the initiation of girls.

Institutions and non-governmental organisations which deal with responsible parenthood and which help teenage mothers should be given more assistance by both the government and the communities where they work, in order to enable them to reach their goals. Among other activities, they should produce easy-to-read materials on the socio-cultural issues of adolescence, some anatomical facts, as well as fertility management and the relevant laws.

References

SIDA Health Division, 1994.

Biographies of the authors

Virginia Kainamula, born 1953
M.Sc. (biology), M.A. (counselling)
Counselling programme co-ordinator for Responsible
Parenthood Education for Youth Project
Member of IDSWSG (Institute of Development Studies Women's
Study Group) at the University of Dar es Salaam, as well as of
YWCA and AAWORD
Married with children

Rosalia Sam Katapa, born 1949
M.Sc. (mathematics and statistics), University of Carleton
Ph.D. (statistics) University of Toronto
Senior lecturer in statistics at the University of Dar es Salaam.
Member of WRDP (Women's Research Documentation Project),
University of Dar es Salaam
Married with three sons

Betty Komba-Malekela, born 1955 in Nachingwea
Grade A teaching certificate. Member of WRDP
Married with six children

Rita Liljeström, born 1928 in Finland
Personal professorship in sociology at the Swedish Council for
Research in the Humanities and Social Sciences
She works at the Department of Sociology, University of
Gothenburg
Married with ten grandchildren

Juliana Chediel Mziray, born 1949
Diploma in office management
Self-employed in business and farming
Researcher at IDSWSG
Church Youth Advisor and Sunday School teacher
Married with four children

Mary Ntukula, born 1956 in Songea
B.A. (sociology and labour law)
M.A. (sociology and manpower planning) at the University of
Dar es Salaam
Manpower development and administrative manager at the
National Steel Corporation Ltd, Dar es Salaam
Member of IDSWSG
Married with five children

Grace Khwaya Puja, born 1948 in Singida
M.A. (education), University of Dar es Salaam and
M.Sc. (library science), University of Southern California
Medical librarian, University of Dar es Salaam
WHO-consultant
Member of WRDP
Married with four children

Alice K. Rugumyamheto, born 1948
B.A. (education) at the University of Dar es Salaam
M.A (education) at San José State University, California
Principal curriculum developer/editor researcher at Tanzania
Institite of Education
Member of IDSWSG
Married with three children

Magdalena Kamugisha Rwebangira, born 1953 in Bukoba
Lawyer and one of the founding members of Tanzania Women
Lawyers' Association
Member of WRDP, as well as of the International Women's
Rights Action Watch (IWRAW) network
Current National Coordinator for Women and Law in East
Africa (Tanzania)
Has recently started her own legal practice
Married and a mother of three

Mary Shuma, born 1953 in Moshi
Master's degree in geography
Moved from teaching geography and economics in secondary
school to the Institite of Curriculum Development
Currently working with the World Wildlife Fund (WWF),
coordinating an Environmental Education Programme for
Tanzania
Member of WRDP
Mother of three

Zubeida Tumbo-Masabo, born 1952 in Songea
Doctorate in Applied Linguistics and Senior Research Fellow,
Institute of Kiswahili Research, University of Dar es Salaam,
specializing in terminology, lexicography and translation
Founding member of WRDP and its current convenor
Coordinator of Teenage Girls and Reproductive Health Study
Group since 1990
Married and a mother of four